WICKER FURNITURE

WICKER FURNITURE

A Guide to Restoring & Collecting

Richard Saunders

CROWN PUBLISHERS, INC. ◂ ▸ NEW YORK

Victorian rockers, left to right: An old peacock design, which is commonly reproduced today; an ornate rocker from the 1880s; a gentleman's rocker with thick serpentine rolled arms and skirting, which frames the entire piece; a lady's rocker with thick braiding, which nevertheless forms graceful lines.

Photograph credits appear on page 241.

Published by Crown Publishers, Inc., 201 East 50th Street, New York, New York 10022
CROWN is a trademark of Crown Publishers, Inc.

Originally published in different form as *Collecting & Restoring Wicker Furniture* by Crown Publishers, Inc. in 1976.

Manufactured in the United States of America

Library of Congress Cataloging-in-Publication Data

Saunders, Richard, 1947–
    Wicker furniture / A guide to Restoring & Collecting—Richard Saunders.—
    [Rev. ed.]
        p.   cm.
    Includes index.
    1. Wicker furniture.   2. Furniture—Repairing.   I. Title.
    II. Title: Wicker furniture.
    TT197.7.S38   1990
    749.213—dc20
    ISBN 0-517-57185-4   89-28351

Book design by Deborah Kerner

10 9 8 7 6 5 4 3 2 1
Revised Edition

For **Paula**

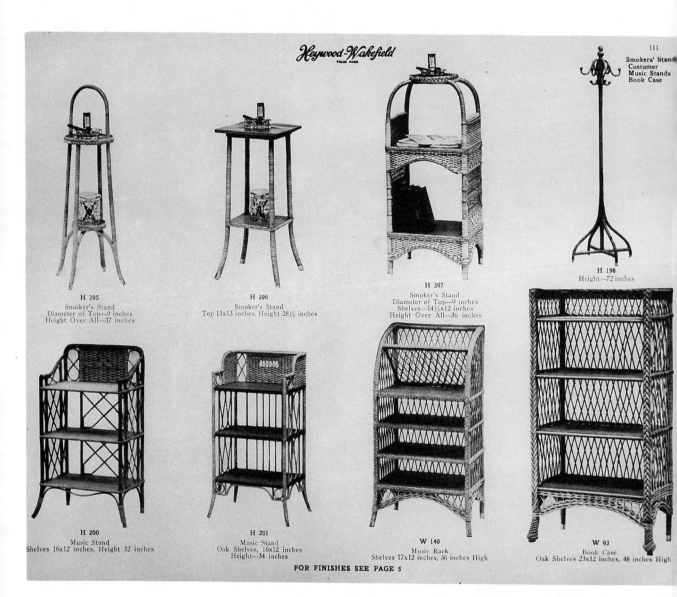

Heywood-Wakefield
TRADE MARK

Smokers' Stand
Costumer
Music Stands
Book Case

H 395
Smoker's Stand
Diameter of Top—9 inches
Height Over All—37 inches

H 396
Smoker's Stand
Top 13x13 inches, Height 28½ inches

H 397
Smoker's Stand
Diameter of Top—9 inches
Shelves—14½x12 inches
Height Over All—36 inches

H 198
Height—72 inches

H 200
Music Stand
Shelves 16x12 inches, Height 32 inches

H 201
Music Stand
Oak Shelves, 16x12 inches
Height—34 inches

W 140
Music Rack
Shelves 17x12 inches, 36 inches High

W 93
Book Case
Oak Shelves 23x12 inches, 48 inches High

FOR FINISHES SEE PAGE 5

*Various wicker pieces from the
1927 Heywood-Wakefield catalog.*

CONTENTS

Color insert appears after page 118

WICKER FURNITURE

INTRODUCTION

In the last twenty years there has been a curious renaissance in the popularity of old wicker furniture in America. Although some of this wicker is accepted as genuine antique furniture, especially those pieces produced during the Victorian era, most pre-1930 wicker is considered "collectible" even if it has not yet achieved true "antique" status. Semantics aside, these masterfully woven wonders of a bygone era are now poised for flight to a far higher level of popularity and critical acceptance than ever before.

Antique wicker furniture is imaginative, daring, and often experimental in design. It is airy, fresh, open, and light. It can be eccentric, seductively romantic, or pragmatic, and down-to-earth. It can possess an aura of Victorian elegance, evoke exotic foreign images, or conjure up nostalgic memories of lazy summer days on a shady country porch. It can be amazingly versatile, but it's never wishy-washy. Wicker has something definite to say to everyone: it creates a mood.

A unique functional art form that has been grossly underrated for decades, quality antique wicker furniture is now being saved, restored, collected, and—most important—appreciated. While the current revival of wicker furniture seems to have been fathered by a number of things, it is safe to say that interior designers have played a major role by their increased use of it. Other factors that have contributed to the comeback of wicker are the nationwide trend toward nostalgia and the collecting of antiques. Too, the growing interest in crafts during the late sixties and into the seventies and eighties has renewed general interest in the craft of wickerwork, thereby leading to a true appreciation of the fine craftsmanship that went into antique wicker furniture. Also, imported reproductions of fancy Victorian-style wicker furniture made in the Orient have aroused public interest in what the original designs really looked like.

Wicker furniture was popular in America from around the close of the Civil War to the late twenties. Then, almost overnight, it was considered gauche and suddenly disappeared from living rooms, dining rooms, bedrooms, porches, and sun-rooms all across the country. Some was stowed away in attics, but much was simply consigned to the junkyard. Today not only is wicker furniture gaining in popularity daily, but most of the pre-1900 pieces have become valuable collector's items, as have some of the better later pieces.

The whimsical individuality that radiates from the handmade wicker produced between 1860 and 1930 has justifiably attracted serious collectors. Its potential both as a decorative element and a specialized field worthy of investment has finally been realized. Wicker is now being studied and evaluated like other forms of nineteenth-century furniture. Museums are actively borrowing and purchasing natural, or unpainted, wicker in fine condition, and the terms "rarity" and "original finish" are now being used to classify them.

Today's collector senses the pride of workmanship that flowed through every piece of wicker furniture made by hand between 1850 and 1915. Highly skilled wickerworkers labored two or three days to produce one armchair or rocker and added their own special touch to each and every piece. A tremendous amount of personal satisfaction and pride went into the making of this furniture, and as a result the general public accepted fine wicker on both aesthetic and consumer levels.

An extremely rare 1880 wicker settee manufactured by the Wakefield Rattan Company.

1
A WORD ABOUT WICKER

Before discussing the history of wicker furniture, it is important first to define the term "wicker." The word is believed to be of Scandinavian origin: from the Swedish *wika,* "to bend," and *vikker,* "willow." Wicker is not a material in itself, as many believe, but rather a very general classification covering all woven furniture. Webster defines wicker as "a small pliant twig," but in reality "wicker" has evolved into an umbrella term covering such materials as rattan, cane, reed, willow, raffia, fiber, rush, and various dried grasses. Surprisingly, the term "wicker" came into widespread use only after the turn of the century. Before that time the old trade catalogs containing what we would now call wicker furniture used the terms "rattan" and "reed" to describe their furniture.

The largest amount of material used in the making of wicker furniture is derived from rattan, a climbing palm native to the East Indies. There are several hundred species of rattan, all characterized by long fibrous stalks with a hard flinty coating. Actually, this plant is more like a vine than a palm, for it winds its way up neighboring trees by means of stout reversed thorns on the leaves, and attains a height of five to six hundred feet without exceeding an inch and a half in diameter. Most of the rattan used for commercial purposes comes from the Far East and Southeast Asia, with the finest variety, *Calamus rotang,* growing

Double heart-shaped back panels dominate this fine 1880s settee.

The rattan palm after the leaves are removed.

◄ 5 ►

A Victorian corner chair with hand-caned back panel and reed loop design.

chiefly in Borneo and the Malay Archipelago, where it thrives in the jungles and swamps.

After the wild rattan is cut, the thorny leaves are removed, leaving a thin-jointed, highly polished cane that resembles young bamboo. While rattan is not related to bamboo, they are sometimes confused; it should be remembered that rattan is a solid growth and bamboo is hollow. The long vines are cut into sections, which vary in length according to the species, and collected by traders for shipment. Rattan is so strong that the Orientals make rope from it that is used as cables for moorings and even suspension bridges. Some of the species are thick enough to be used as walking canes; in fact, the word "rattan" is from the Malayan *rotan,* "walking stick." Rattan's ability to bend without breaking and its glossy, water-resistant surface make it useful for outdoor furniture.

When rattan is split, the outer bark is sliced off in long, thin strips to make cane—that resilient material used in weaving openwork seats and backs for chairs. The inner bark, or pith, of rattan is called "reed." Unlike rattan, reed can be easily stained or painted any color; it is widely used in wicker furniture because of its extraordinary pliability. The reed derived from the rattan palm (not to be confused with swamp reed, which was often used in ancient wicker furniture) was first used in the manufacture of wicker furniture during the 1850s.

Other materials used in wicker furniture are often confused with rattan and reed. One of them is willow. The highly pliable twigs from willow trees (sometimes called "osiers") are soft but tough, and take a good stain. Raffia, also used in wicker furniture, is a rather coarse fiber cut from the leafstalks of the raphia palm in Madagascar. Fiber (sometimes called "art fibre" or "fibre-reed") came into wide use during World War I as a new material for wicker furniture. It is made of machine-twisted paper that has been chemically treated. This material is usually soft and pliable, but some types are stiff because the paper is twisted around a flexible wire center for greater strength. To a lesser extent, rush, a perennial plant that is a member of the sedge family, and various dried grasses, such as sea grass and prairie grass, have also been used in wicker furniture.

Although the majority of antique wicker furniture is made of rattan, reed, or willow, many pieces were made by combining two or three of these materials; the craftsman realized that some material lent itself better to fancy scrollwork and others to simple weaving and wrapping.

The rattan palm (Calamus rotang) *grows wild in the East Indies.*

2
Early Wickerwork Furniture

Older than cloth weaving and pottery making, the weaving of twigs and swamp reed into wickerwork goes back as far as the chipping of flints into arrowheads by Neolithic man.

The oldest surviving pieces of wicker furniture date back to the Egyptian empire. Because of the preserving effect of sand, the extremely dry atmosphere in that area, and the superior tombs, it is chiefly in Egypt that ancient wickerwork furniture has survived in such an excellent state after being buried for centuries. Having had a fine basketry tradition using the local palm, grasses, and rush since 4000 B.C., the ancient Egyptians gradually developed and expanded this craft until they could construct larger wickerwork items such as coffins made of coiled rush and chests made of swamp reed. Around 2000 B.C. woven reed cosmetic boxes took the place of the heavier, more elaborate chests of wood used for the same purpose. One of the finest surviving examples of this early wickerwork is a toilet chest that was found in fine condition at the burial site of Queen Menuthotep at Thebes.

The Cairo Museum has a reed and papyrus chest from Thebes that was unearthed at the tomb of Yuia and Thuiu. According to Hollis S. Baker, a well-known authority on ancient furniture, this chest,

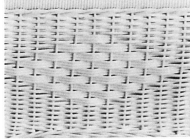

Ancient and turn of the century weaves.

Sumerian statue of the steward Ebih-il seated on a wicker hassock (c. 2600 B.C.).

Egyptian wig box made of reed and papyrus (c. 1400 B.C.).

which is obviously an ancestor of the summer "reed" furniture of today, served a very special purpose. It contained the wigs of the lady Thuiu, who, following the customs of the day, had her head shaved for hygienic reasons; she consequently needed a suitable place to keep these important adjuncts to her wardrobe. The general construction of the chest and the wrapping of the joints between the stretchers and the legs of the chest anticipate the methods used in the making of reed and cane furniture at the present time. The little openings in the sides resemble the barred windows of a house and give the chest an architectural look—a popular device of Egyptian cabinet-makers, who often designed chests with sides resembling the facades of houses.

From the Sumerian civilization at Mari, in northeastern Syria, comes one of the earliest pieces of evidence attesting to the existence of wicker

Egyptian chest made of reed and rush (c. 1600 B.C.).

An Art Deco armchair with drink holder and magazine pocket built into the armrests.

furniture: a sculpture of the steward Ebih-il sitting on a round hassock of woven reed dating back to 2600 B.C. Sumerian furniture made of reed, which was readily available from the marshes of southern Mesopotamia, was made around the same time the first furniture appeared in Egypt. But, unlike Egyptian furniture, the remaining Early Dynastic Mesopotamian furniture consists only of a few fragments of ornamentation.

> In both cases furnishings were placed in the tombs of important persons at the time of the burials; but in Egypt the early tombs were protected by massive structures of masonry which still stand above the desert sand, whereas in Mesopotamia the tombs were constructed in a less permanent manner and the walls built of mud and brick have mostly disintegrated and disappeared from the landscape.

Still considered the greatest archaeological discovery of all time, the unearthing of the tomb of Egyptian king Tutankamen from the fourteenth century B.C. created headlines around the world. Lord Carnarvon and his American assistant, Howard Carter, crawled through the black passageways of Rameses VI's tomb holding candles, which ultimately shed light on fantastic artifacts. Stunning alabaster art, jeweled statues, elaborate gilt couches, and the gold inner coffin bearing the likeness of the boy king had miraculously survived the ravages of time in the airtight tomb. Of course, these amazing finds overshadowed the more modest and utilitarian artifacts. Among the more practical, everyday objects were wicker stools made of swamp reed, wicker boxes, and mats woven from rush.

Stone relief showing a Roman woman seated in a wicker chair remarkably similar in design to those in use today. Early third century A.D.

The different climatic conditions in southern Europe account for the absence of any wickerwork relics similar to those found in the Egyptian tombs. The antiquity of wicker furniture from the Greek civilization is known only by carvings on stone, yet not only have stone carvings of Roman Empire wickerwork survived, but written accounts by Roman authors tell us that wicker furniture was plentiful around the time of Christ. Some of these pieces exhibit methods of construction (such as

under-and-over weaving techniques, joints wrapped with flat reed, and open latticework) that were used in making wicker furniture two thousand years later.

In Rome the ancient art of wattling (a basic type of wickerwork using sticks intertwined with willow twigs) was practiced for centuries. Willows were cultivated largely for the making of baskets, chariotlike carts, and furniture. Pliny, in dealing with the cultivation of these willows and their use, wrote:

> . . . other willows throw out osiers of remarkable thinness, adapted by their suppleness and graceful slenderness for the manufacture of wicker-work. Others again, of a stouter make, are used for weaving panniers, and many other utensils employed in agriculture; while from a whiter willow the bark is peeled off, and being remarkably tractable, admits of various utensils being of it, which require a softer and more pliable material than leather: this last is also found particularly useful in the construction of those articles of luxury, reclining chairs.

Turn of the century rocker with closely woven backrest and rolled arms.

The principle behind the fabrication of wickerwork furniture was simple enough: the material was woven in such a way that it was yielding and extremely comfortable to sit in because it would bend and give with the weight of the body. Thus, the ancient woven chair had much in common with a piece of basketry, for it was woven in the exact same way and possessed the same qualities of lightness and flexibility.

The Roman invasion of the first century B.C. brought Britain into contact with the continent, and by the time the Romans withdrew, in the fifth century A.D., the British had inherited the wicker chair. Although British traditions in wickerwork date back to the early Iron Age (through the ancient craft of basketmaking), the Britons' first contact with wickerwork furniture was through Roman wicker chairs like the one depicted in the Romano-British sepulchral monument to Julia Velva. The craft of basketmaking survived the overall decay of skill that accompanied the fall of the Western Roman Empire in A.D. 476, and the scope of early British basketmaking widened to include "basket chairs" made of peeled willow twigs or woven rush. Designed with comfort in mind, these chairs employed circular, full-skirted bases and gently sloped backrests. The basket chair was used by the common people throughout medieval times; the more important members of

A figure is shown sitting in a wicker chair at the left of this Romano-British sepulchral monument to Julia Velva. Third century A.D.

society sat on huge wooden thrones. Interestingly, although the design of these thrones had improved by the close of the medieval period, the simple basket chairs of the peasants were probably much more comfortable.

By the sixteenth century the wicker chair was a "people's chair" because of its low price, unpretentiousness, and immunity to changes of fashion. In 1569 the Basket Makers Guild was established in London, and it was probably from this fraternal organization that most of the wicker furniture of that period came. Unfortunately, most of its records were destroyed in the Great Fire of 1666.

Wickerwork enjoyed a long reign of popularity in Britain, and even found its way into the writings of Shakespeare, Robert Burns, Charles Dickens, and Henry Fielding. An early literary reference to basket chairs (sometimes referred to as "twiggen" or "beehive" chairs) appears in the sixteenth-century "Elegie I, On Jealosie" by John Donne:

> Nor when he swolne, and pamper'd with great fare
> Sits downe, and snorts, cag'd in his basket chaire.

In sixteenth-century France the term *guérite* (sentry box) was given to a particular style of wicker armchair with an extremely high, rounded back that curved forward at the top to form a hood. Probably designed for the elderly, it afforded protection against drafts and from sunlight when used outdoors. The design used deep wings that helped form the arched canopy, and was still being reproduced as late as the early 1900s by some of America's leading wicker furniture companies. A similar type of hooded woven "wykyr" chair is mentioned in English farm inventories as early as 1571. Further evidence of the hooded wicker chair can be found in a seventeenth-century painting by the Flemish artist and pupil of Rubens, Jacob Jordaens.

By this time wickerwork was made around the globe. In countries with warmer climates, rattan, cane, swamp reed, various fibers, twisted palm leaves, and young bamboo were put to use, while colder countries employed rush, wild grasses, willow twigs, roots, and split wood strips.

A wicker chair appears in this seventeenth-century painting, **The Holy Family,** *by Jacob Jordaens. Note the birdcage also.*

The oldest known piece of American wickerwork came to the New World on the *Mayflower* in 1620. Legend has it that this wicker cradle was used to rock Peregrine White to sleep on the long voyage across the Atlantic. The exact origin of the piece is shrouded in mystery, and it will probably never be known for certain whether it was made in Holland or imported by the Dutch from China. The latter may be more realistic. Trade between China and Western Europe commenced following the Portuguese establishment of a permanent settlement in 1557 at Macao, not far from present-day Hong Kong. Regardless of the true origin of this famous cradle (now housed at the Pilgrim Hall Museum in Plymouth, Massachusetts), the fact remains that early American wicker furniture played a very minor role in the lives of the colonists.

Many American Indian tribes were expert basketmakers long before any whites came to America, yet the Indians never felt a need to produce wicker furniture. The settlers, on the other hand, brought with them the memory of simple European wicker furniture, such as the straw beehive chairs of England, and they were soon making their own; the proof can be found in many seventeenth-century American wills and inventories of household goods. One of the earliest of these documents, a will dated February 1639–40, comes from a Captain Adam Thoroughgood of Princess Anne County, Virginia, who listed "one chair of wicker for a child" with the furniture in Mrs. Thoroughgood's chamber. In another account, dated 1666, an indentured servant, George Alsop of Maryland, wrote of New Englanders whose vessels brought mostly "Medera-Wines, Sugars, Salt, Wicker-Chairs, and Tin Candle-sticks."

Early in the 1660s, during the reign of Charles II, rattan was imported into England by the East India Company during the beginning years of the China trade. The glossy cane (the outside of rattan) was used extensively in weaving the backs and seats of wooden chairs, but the center of the rattan (reed) was merely treated as waste. When it was first used, the cane was wide and bulky, but by the end of the seventeenth century it had been reduced in size, and shortly thereafter

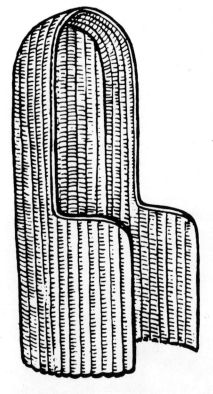

The French guérite, a sixteenth-century hooded wicker chair.

chairs with very fine cane seats were being produced in England and France.

Around the time England assumed the lead in the China trade, in the mid-eighteenth century, the Chinese made Canton the only port open to foreign trade. The trading season at Canton usually lasted about six months, from midsummer to midwinter, but it was often cut short because of the onslaught of the unpredictable monsoon season. More obstacles arose when Western traders came under constant surveillance by the Chinese police because of a surge in opium sales. Westerners were restricted to doing business at private residences and at trading headquarters called "hongs." The hongs were owned by the wealthier merchants of Canton, and one of the most coveted honors foreign traders could be given was to be invited to soirées at the homes of these merchants. It was here, in the lavish homes of successful Chinese merchants, that British and American traders first set eyes on elaborate wicker fantail, or peacock, chairs made of rattan. Many of the chairs were decorated with jewels woven into the fantail backrest, creating the illusion of shining peacock feathers.

By the mid-nineteenth century the China trade had changed considerably for American traders. With the opening of the treaty ports of Hong Kong, Shanghai, Amoy, Foochow, and Ning-po early in the 1840s, the traders began to frequent ports other than Canton and were offered a greater variety of goods. The most important item shipped back to America was neither expensive silks nor exquisite pieces of porcelain, but a rough material used exclusively for securing cargo during the turbulent ocean voyage. The material, whole rattan, would shortly become the building block of a giant American industry for decades to come.

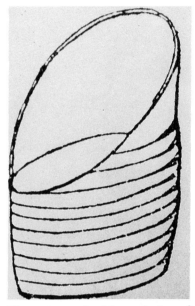

The straw beehive chair of seventeenth- and eighteenth-century England.

3

THE GOLDEN AGE OF WICKER

While the strong association of wicker furniture and exotic foreign countries played a major role in establishing wicker's popularity in the Victorian era, the industry actually was born on American soil and not (as so many people still insist on believing) in the Orient. This widespread misconception may have been nurtured by the fact that the rattan palm grows wild in the Far East. Also adding to the general confusion is the abundance of the poor-quality wicker reproductions from the Orient that have been imported into this country for the past forty years. Ironically, these reproductions are based on American Victorian wicker designs.

By the early 1840s, after the new ports for foreign trade had opened up in China, it was common practice for clipper ships sailing between these ports and America to carry rattan on board as dunnage, to prevent the cargo from shifting. One day in 1844, while watching a vast quantity of rattan being dumped out on the docks in Boston, a young grocer named Cyrus Wakefield picked up one of the long, odd-looking poles and examined it carefully. Amazed at its flexibility, he joined a group of volunteers who were carting the rattan off the docks because it constituted a fire hazard. After collecting an armful of the poles, Wakefield went home and began an experiment by wrapping a provincial-style chair with the discarded rattan.

Cyrus Wakefield I (1811–73).

The Wakefield clipper ship Hoogly discharging a cargo of rattan at Constitution Wharf, Boston.

The original Rattan logo from the Wakefield Rattan Company.

Quickly realizing the great untapped potential of rattan, but having no formal training in furniture making, young Wakefield quit the grocery business and embarked on what proved to be a highly profitable jobbing trade in rattan. Selling his initial purchases of imported rattan to basketmakers and furniture manufacturers (who used the outer covering, cane, to weave chair seats), he found his jobbing trade quite lucrative. The demand for cane for chair seats was increasing rapidly in America (it had been used for this purpose in Europe as early as the seventeenth century). As luck would have it, Wakefield had a brother-in-law in the house of Messrs. Russell & Company in Canton, China, to whom he wrote and sent samples of the cane most in demand by furniture manufacturers. Wakefield knew that if he could obtain cane from China, he could bypass the largest problem in the rattan business: that of employing workers to hand strip the cane from whole rattan, a very slow and costly task. The correspondence proved successful. Within a few years he was hiring ships to bring rattan and cane back to Boston, and his importations became well known throughout the United States. During these early years Wakefield also continued with his experiments, designing increasingly ornate pieces of rattan furniture in the Victorian style.

According to Lilley Eaton, it was around mid-century when

> . . . a fortunate speculation gave him [Wakefield] both credit and capital, so that he could enlarge his business. Learning that there were several large lots of rattan in the New York market, the article at this time being much depressed, Mr. Wakefield, with all the ready money he could command, went to that city, established his quarters quietly at the Astor House, and put his brokers at work to obtain the lowest price at which the entire stock could be purchased, enjoining upon them not to name the purchaser. Having obtained the desired information, he decided to take all the available lots, for which he paid sufficient cash to make the material subject to his order. This gave him the whole control of the rattan stock of the country. Prices soon advanced, and he was enabled to sell, so that he realized a handsome profit. This single operation not only put money and credit at his disposal, but also gave him a prestige in the business, which he ever after maintained.

In an effort to increase furniture production, Wakefield and his wife left Boston to establish the Wakefield Rattan Company in South Reading, Massachusetts, in 1855. Since the factory was situated along the rushing Mill River, waterpower soon took the place of hand power, and before long steam was added as a power source to split the rattans, which were brought to South Reading from the Boston docks; the finished furniture was taken back to Boston in horse-drawn wagons. Most of Wakefield's early wicker furniture was made by combining rattan, cane (usually wrapped around a hardwood frame), and locally grown willow.

As Cyrus Wakefield's import business became known throughout the United States, he continued experimenting with wicker furniture, creating original designs from frames of hickory or oak. After steaming and bending the wood into flowing shapes, he filled in the frames with rattan fancywork and wrapped them with split cane. The laborers for his new factory were local townspeople and workers who had arrived in the Boston area in increasing numbers during and after the potato famine in Ireland. By 1870 these people made up a large percentage of the labor force. Wicker furniture making was quickly being transformed from a homemade craft into a sophisticated, highly profitable industry.

By the 1850s wicker furniture had caught on with a limited number of other furniture makers in the United States. The work of New York designer John Topf even made it across the Atlantic, displayed at the Crystal Palace, home of London's Great Exposition of 1851. This is one of the earliest illustrations of American wicker furniture on record, reproduced from the "art-journal" catalog of the exposition. The chair received a considerable amount of attention, especially from the furniture designers of the day, who felt that the Victorian revival of the French Rococo style of the seventeenth and eighteenth centuries lent itself particularly well to the medium of wicker—motifs combining elaborate curves, shell forms, C-scrolls, and cabriole legs were easily and effectively adapted.

Gervase Wheeler's *Rural Homes,* a taste manual published in New York in 1852, pictured these illustrations. All this furniture was from the warerooms of Messrs. J. & C. Berrian of New York, who Wheeler claimed were the most extensive manufacturers of wicker furniture at that time. In the article Wheeler explained:

> . . . the wood of which the frames for the chairs, etc., are made is white oak or hickory, and is, in the first instance, selected with great care so that the grain may be straight. After being steamed to soften it, it is bent

An early-Victorian wicker garden chair from the Crystal Palace Exposition of 1851.

CANE FURNITURE.

Sofa, Arm Chair, Arm Chair with Rockers, and Fo

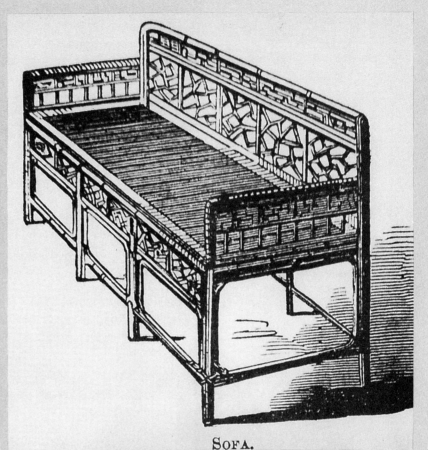

SOFA.

From Gervase Wheeler's Rural Homes

A wicker settee in the Chinese style (above), made of whole rattan in such a way as to simulate the look of bamboo.

Wicker "sofa," armchair, rocking chair, and foot bench (left). Wheeler felt that the so-called sofa, because of the pointed termination of its curves, approached the gothic principle of construction.

A sturdy wicker armchair (right) with wrapped-cane frame, reed fancy-work and cane seat.

CHAIR.

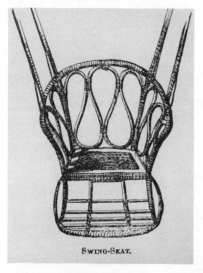

Unique child's swing seat with footrest and cane seat.

into the required forms and allowed to dry, so that it may not shrink or start out of shape after it has been made up . . . the cane itself (rattan, as it is properly called) is split, where it is bound on the framework—some pieces of furniture show the wood in its undivided state . . . the principal excellencies of cane as a material for chairs, sofas, baskets, etc., etc., are its durability, elasticity, and great facility of being turned and twisted into an almost endless variety of shapes; hence in chairs, there is every assistance given by it in obtaining that greatest of all luxuries—an easy seat and a springy back.

Wheeler also mentioned that at least two thousand girls were employed in a rattan manufactory in the Bloomingdale section of New York City, and that the House of Refuge in New York State employed three to four hundred boys in the production of wicker furniture.

Workstand for a sewing room and flower stand with a metal liner for holding water or wet sand.

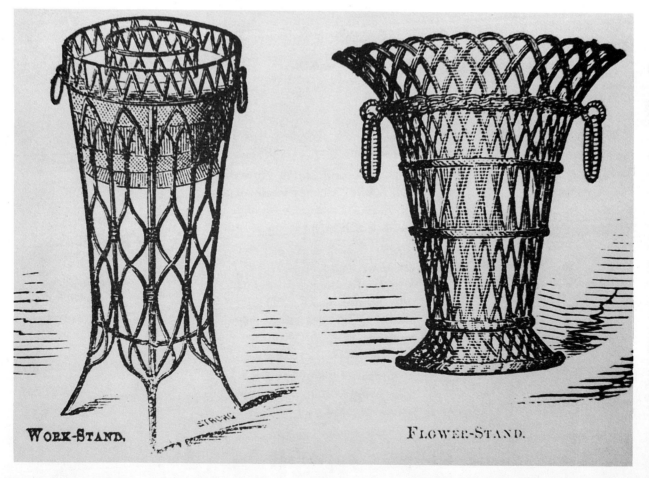

CHAIR.

FIRE-SCREEN.

Fire screen made of rattan.

CRIB, OR STANDARD BED-STEAD.

Wicker crib with a wrapped-cane
arch as a canopy.

Lady's armchair with flowing,
delicate lines.

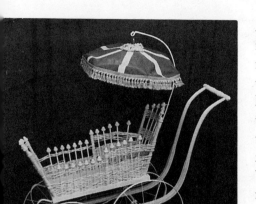

An 1880s doll buggy with wooden "acorn" beadwork attached to the vertical spokes and the original canvas parasol intact.

Another company to come out of this period had its roots in the thriving industrial empire of Samuel Colt, who also perfected and produced the repeating revolver. Colt built his sprawling munitions plant in 1854, less than two miles from the center of Hartford, Connecticut. Because the location was subject to annual floods, Colt constructed a dike nearly two miles long, planted with willows to hold the soil in place. Since the willow shoots had to be cut back annually, Colt used the willow crop for the manufacture of wicker furnishings; the Colt Willow Ware Works was added to the armory complex in the late 1850s. Approximately one hundred German workers were employed in the factory at the start of the Civil War, forty being experienced basketmakers and master craftsmen from Potsdam. Colt had to import virtually an entire community because the willow workers had refused to leave without their families. As an incentive, he had a reproduction of their German hamlet built in Hartford, ready for them upon their arrival. Unfortunately, the wicker factory burned down in 1873, and the production of wicker furniture never resumed.

English wicker chairs of the mid-1850s stood in direct contrast to the ornate, flowing designs being produced in America. The basket chair developed in medieval times remained the traditional design for wicker furniture, with few changes other than the tendency to use open-plaited skirting on the lower half of the chair. A slight variation of the basket chair, which began to emerge around this time, eventually became known as the croquet chair. It was similar in shape to the basket chair, the major difference being its greater size. Both these chairs remained very popular in Britain throughout the nineteenth century.

In 1856 the Taiping Rebellion (an outgrowth of the Opium War) temporarily cut off the supply of rattan from China. Cyrus Wakefield and his assistant, an inventive Scot named William Houston, began to devise ways to use the waste products of rattan already in stock, and soon developed a way to spin the shavings into yarn, from which mats were made. Through the years Houston produced woven floor coverings, window shades, and table mats. In 1866 he developed the first brush mat ever made of rattan, and four years later he invented a loom to weave cane webbing, which was soon to become very popular for covering seats in railroad and street-railway cars.

While Houston's weaving experiments continued, Cyrus Wakefield

The traditional English basket chair of the mid-1850s.

This photograph of a wicker-filled porch in 1890s Atlanta invites you to sit down and relax in the shade.

became obsessed with trying to find a way to use still more of the rattan, for up until this point the inner pith, called "reed," was still treated as waste. After years of experimentation Wakefield began using reed in the construction of frames for hoop skirts, and soon after he was using reed for wicker furniture. He found it far more pliable than rattan, and also capable of taking a good stain and paint, whereas rattan could only be lacquered.

The discovery of reed as a valuable furniture material necessitated a more rapid and economical method than hand stripping the cane from the reed. The American Rattan Company of Fitchburg, Massachusetts, was the only concern that cut cane by machine, but their methods were outdated. Their emphasis was on stripping off the glossy cane for the purpose of creating wooden chair seating, rather than on stripping the cane away to get to the newly discovered material, reed. Crude cane-splitting machines powered by water were followed by a steam-driven machine patented in 1861 by Thomas Mayall (assignor to Cyrus Wakefield). A new era dawned in wicker furniture production.

Throughout the Civil War years furniture manufacturers realized more and more how extremely well suited to Victorian designs wicker was, and they wasted no time in capitalizing on this. From wicker furniture's first appearance on the marketplace, nineteenth-century Americans fell in love with it. It perfectly captured the mood of the times. Pre-1900 wicker added an uncommon blend of informality and dimension to any room in the home. The elusive qualities of wicker somehow captured the leisurely pace of the day, while at the same time adding a touch of exotic Oriental mystery.

Victorian wicker furniture was eclectic, an odd mixture of progressive and traditional designs drawn from innumerable sources and combined with motifs of several different periods. Experimentation became all-important, and wicker furniture was pushed toward new horizons in design, horizons that seemed limitless because of the flexibility of the newly discovered reed and the relatively new and growing influence of Victorian styles in America. In fact, wicker furniture seemed like a natural for Victorian designs, for it combined materials (rattan, reed, cane, willow twigs, and so on) just as the Victorians combined styles (Rococo, Classical, Elizabethan, Gothic, Chinese, Italian Renaissance).

While the majority of wicker furniture made between 1865 and 1880 was intended for indoor use, during this period it also became very

Levi Heywood.

fashionable as garden and porch furniture. When wealthy Americans made their annual summer migrations to exclusive seaside resorts or mountain retreats, they gradually noticed more and more wicker-filled verandas, sleeping porches, and gazebos. Usually left in its natural state or lightly stained, wicker furniture was lightweight and able to withstand the weather year round. Many manufacturers recommended leaving dry or brittle pieces of wicker in the rain, for water restored the elastic quality so admired in this furniture.

After the Civil War it became apparent to the citizens of South Reading that better town facilities were needed, especially a new town hall. Wakefield, by this time not only a wealthy and well-established businessman but also the town's leading citizen, rose to the occasion by donating more than $120,000 for the purpose. The local citizenry were so overcome by his generous gesture that they voted to change the name of the town to honor him, and on July 1, 1868, South Reading became Wakefield, Massachusetts.

Cyrus Wakefield's rattan business was so successful that by the early 1870s his manufactories and storehouses spanned ten acres of floorage. Then, during a financial crash known as the Panic of '73, Wakefield incorporated the Wakefield Rattan Company. He died of a heart attack just two weeks later, on October 26, 1873. Although he had large holdings in both real estate and railroad stocks, Cyrus Wakefield died bankrupt, and his widow, whose father had left a large estate, paid his debts so that his financial condition would not appear in the town's probate records.

Although Cyrus Wakefield left no children, he had a nephew and namesake, Cyrus Wakefield II. Young Cyrus had served as a representative of the Wakefield Company in Singapore since 1865. Upon his uncle's death he returned home to assume the responsibilities of managing the company. Less than two years later the newly elected company president acquired the American Rattan Company, for years a chief competitor of the Wakefield Rattan Company. By that time the national economy had greatly improved, and the Wakefield plant prospered once again.

Shortly before his death Cyrus Wakefield had started to sell rattan to Levi Heywood, founder of Heywood Brothers and Company, established in 1861. Heywood's interest in furniture making went back to 1826, when he had begun the manufacture of wooden chairs in his home town of Gardner, Massachusetts. In the 1840s Heywood devoted his attention to the construction of machinery for making furniture and invented, among other things, a combination of three machines for splitting, shaving, and otherwise manipulating rattan. One of Heywood's most remarkable inventions was a machine for bending wood, which caused Francis Thonet of Vienna (son of the creator of the most highly acclaimed bentwood furniture ever produced and head of the largest chair manufacturing plant in the world at that time) to write, after a visit to the Heywood factory: "I must tell you candidly that you have the best machinery for bending wood that I ever saw, and I will say that I have seen and experimented a great deal in the bending of wood."

Lady's armchair from the 1880s, made by the Wakefield Rattan Company.

Like Cyrus Wakefield, Levi Heywood had an inventive genius at his disposal, in the person of Gardner A. Watkins. After producing several power looms that could weave cane into continuous sheets, Watkins invented an automatic channeling machine that could cut a groove around the wooden seat of a chair, thereby allowing the edges of this sheet cane (as it has come to be called) to be pressed into the groove and fastened tight by means of a triangular-shaped reed called "spline." When these two inventions were combined and put to use, the results were dramatic. No longer were hand caners hired to weave seats. Prewoven, or "set-in," cane seats proved to be much more economical than hand caning.

By 1870 Heywood Brothers and Company, then the largest chair manufacturer in the United States, was bringing in more than one million dollars annually. Shortly thereafter Levi Heywood, thanks in no small measure to the inventions of Gardner A. Watkins, was able to enter the wicker field with significant savings in labor costs. Over the next quarter of a century Heywood's firm would prove to be a fierce competitor with the Wakefield Rattan Company.

In 1876 the Philadelphia Centennial Exhibition featured an international display of the finest arts and crafts of the day. Among the most notable pieces of wicker furniture were the hourglass chairs from China, the last quality wicker furniture to be made for the West.

A slant-back wicker chair with retractable footrest from Ceylon (c. 1870). This type of light-weight chair was in common use aboard passenger ships of the period. The frame was made of bamboo; the material used in the weaving was cane. The wide arm-rests were often put to good use to hold food and drink. This style of chair was also on display in the Chinese pavilion at the Philadelphia Centennial of 1876.

The Wakefield Rattan Company, having recently expanded to the West Coast by establishing a branch office in San Francisco, entered the exhibition and received an award "for original design and superior workmanship in furniture, chairs, and baskets, also for originality in the manufacture of mats and baskets of an otherwise waste material; also for a new form of car seats, durable, cool, clean, and economical." As to the "new form of car seats," Richard N. Greenwood, a great-grandson of Levi Heywood and president of the Heywood-Wakefield Company from 1929 to 1966, reminds us that, several years before Philadelphia's Centennial Exhibition, William Houston of the Wake-field Rattan Company "developed ingenious looms for weaving the cane into a fabric. It was this machinery and skill in weaving long, continuous sheets of cane webbing that put the Wakefield Rattan Company into the railway and street car seating business, for cane was then acknowledged as the best material with which to cover seats of this type."

In the late 1870s wicker chairs from Ceylon with retractable foot-rests and wide arms caught the attention of one British writer, who said: "It seems a pity that sofas and chairs made of straw or bamboo should not be more used than they are. I mean, used as they come from the maker's hands, not painted or gilded, and becushioned and bedizened into hopeless vulgarity. They are only admissible 'au naturel,' and should stand upon their own merits."

Although most wicker furniture at this time was still left in its natural state, there was a growing tendency on the part of the general public to paint wicker, and by the 1880s, when reed had replaced rattan as the material most commonly used for wicker furniture, manufacturers had come to realize that the buying public preferred reed furniture because it could be painted easily. Manufacturers quickly responded to this trend in a more conservative and artistic manner, "judiciously gilding" reeds to highlight designs. This gilding of the lily was accomplished by dyeing or painting individual reeds before weaving them into a piece. Called "fancy colored reeds" in the trade catalogs, the combinations of green, red, white, and gold seemed to jump out at the viewer. An 1883 issue of *Century* magazine featured a Wakefield Rattan Company advertisement that declared, "the new and original idea of color work is having great success, and meets the popular demand for novelty in fall furnishing."

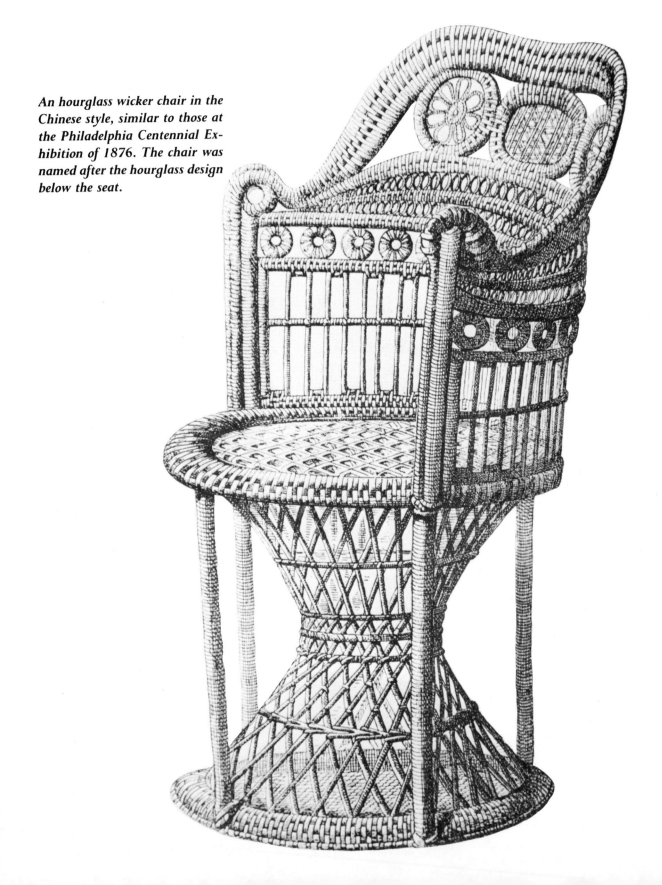

An hourglass wicker chair in the Chinese style, similar to those at the Philadelphia Centennial Exhibition of 1876. The chair was named after the hourglass design below the seat.

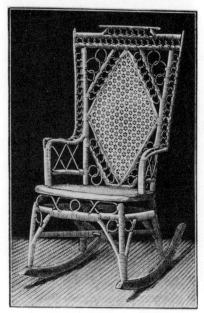

DIAMOND PANEL PATTERN.

No. 412. Ladies' Sitting Chair, $7.00
 " 385. " Rocking " 7.50

During the 1870s Levi Heywood developed a new method of bending rattan to greater extents. This method, adapted from his experiments in wood bending, encouraged wicker furniture manufacturers to experiment with new designs using graceful rattan frames around which narrow strips of flat reed or cane were wrapped. When this new method of bending rattan was coupled with the dramatic fancywork made possible through the use of the pliable reed, the results were truly fantastic. Let's look through some sample pages from the 1881 Wakefield Rattan Company catalog.

Wicker furniture for children began its climb in popularity in the late 1870s because of the nineteenth-century concern for proper ventilation and hygiene. While children's high chairs and cribs were being produced in huge quantities, the darling of the age was the wicker baby carriage. Although the manufacture of wicker baby carriages (also known as perambulators) began during the Civil War, there was little demand for them until the mid-1870s, when Heywood Brothers and Company began turning out quality carriages in large numbers. Offered in a tremendous variety of designs, these carriages were also stained to order (cherry, oak, or mahogany) and came with plush upholstery and a choice of silk or satin parasols. The demand for wicker baby carriages was so enormous between 1880 and 1895 that Heywood Brothers and Company devoted an entire factory to nothing but carriage making.

By this time major wicker companies were also adding specialized items to their baby carriage lines. Many firms ensured their carriages' year-round use: for an extra two dollars, the 1886 Heywood Brothers and Company catalog offered runners to convert any of their carriages into "baby sleighs." Another unique design was the now rare "twin" carriage, designed for two babies, with seats facing each other and employing double parasols. In their 1890 spring trade catalog the

DIAMOND PANEL PATTERN.

No. 413. Gents' Reception Sitting Chair, $8.50
 " 414. " Library Rocking " 9.00
 " 415. " Large Sitting " 10.00
 " 416. " " Rocking " 10.50

The lady's diamond-panel rocker was one of the most popular wicker designs of the Victorian era. The gentleman's version of the same rocker is slightly larger and has diamond-shaped panels under the arms.

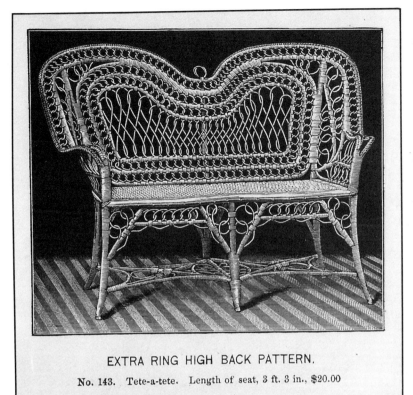

EXTRA RING HIGH BACK PATTERN.

No. 143. Tete-a-tete. Length of seat, 3 ft. 3 in., $20.00

Ornate settee from the Wakefield Rattan Company catalog of 1881.

No. 3. Sitting, $1.50
" 1. Rocker, 1.75

No. 488. Sitting. $3.00
" 487. Rocker, 3.25

Children's wicker from the 1881 Wakefield Rattan Company catalog: rocker with spider-web caned back; rocker with open-work back; rare potty chairs.

No. 496. $5.00

No. 497. $3.00

Victorian conversation chair with
spider-web caned back and caned seats.

Elaborate Victorian swinging
crib. Very rare.

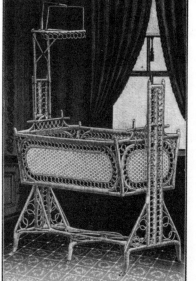

No. 428. Star Panel Swing Crib, $19.00
With Canopy, . 20.00

Gendron Iron Wheel Company of Toledo, Ohio (one of the finest manufacturers of children's wheeled vehicles as well as a large retailer of wicker baby carriages at that time), stated that they could customize any of their seventy-two single-carriage designs "into a twin cab if desired, by adding one-half of the list price on the same."

During the 1880s wicker baby carriages had become so popular that Levi Heywood's company began printing separate trade catalogs for these unique vehicles. The illustrations reproduced here are from the 1886 Heywood Brothers and Company baby carriage catalog.

A hooded reed carriage with runners for winter use. Virtually all the Heywood Brothers baby carriages of this period could be converted into sleighs simply by removing the wheels and putting on runners, which were sold separately by the company.

Victorian hooded baby carriage with an enameled caned body. The upholstery was usually silk or satin, the standard colors were cardinal, wine, gold, light blue, peacock, and brown.

R 124.
Reed Body, Stained Cherry and Varnished.

An extremely ornate Victorian reed carriage with fancy scrollwork. Reed body, stained cherry, varnished.

Reed baby carriage with parasol; Victorian. The body, which resembles an upturned seashell, was stained cherry and varnished at the factory.

R 130.
Reed Body, Stained Cherry and Varnished.

Twin carriages made of reed and stained cherry, as this one is, were produced in limited quantities in the 1880s, and so are understandably rare today. Most carriages then had elliptic front and back springs.

In America the 1880s was perhaps the most important decade in wicker furniture design, for the experiments of the preceding three decades had now been fully developed and perfected by highly skilled craftsmen. During this period the latest rage sweeping the country was Orientalism. After influencing decorative arts such as silver, ceramics, and textiles, it invaded the realm of wicker furniture design. Not surprisingly, the delicate asymmetry of Japanese art found its way into many 1880 designs, most notably in the popular Japanese fan motif set into the back panels of many wicker armchairs and rockers of the era.

Rocker with serpentine arms and scalloped patterns woven into backrest.

The public finally accepted wicker on a large scale once it was realized that the three-dimensional, airy quality of this furniture was equally suited to use indoors and out. As the popularity of wicker continued to grow, many new companies were established with the idea of cashing in on what was thought to be a nationwide trend. Well-established furniture manufacturers also began to include wicker in their showrooms, and in the late 1880s both Sears, Roebuck and Company and Montgomery Ward Company took dead aim at the small-town market, offering inexpensive wicker furniture through their handy mail-order catalogs sent free for the asking. Unfortunately, the workmanship and quality of the materials in their furniture were inferior to those of the pieces produced by older firms specializing in wicker furniture.

Almost all the wicker furniture of this period was varnished or stained at the factories in order to give it a more finished look, but the public's penchant for painting wicker pieces to match a specific décor in the home was stronger than ever. As sunlight and indoor plants invaded the Victorian sitting room, wicker accent pieces made of reed were painted white, dark green, brown, and in some extreme cases gold.

In order to further stimulate sales, a few wicker companies produced special novelty designs that relied on the middle class's unwavering sense of national pride; these included Liberty Bell and American flag motifs woven into backrests. Another successful merchandising gimmick was the issuing of trade cards. These trade cards, about the size of the popular tobacco cards of the 1880–1900 period that featured

Rocker from the 1880s made by the Wakefield Rattan Company.

baseball or theatrical stars, served as company advertisements. Wicker cards displayed attractive catalog illustrations of popular wicker designs, with factory and warehouse locations printed on the reverse side.

For the Wakefield and Heywood Brothers companies, this decade was one of keen competition; as Richard N. Greenwood said in his speech commemorating the 125th anniversary of the Heywood Brothers furniture business: "Both firms grew at about the same rate, both were being managed by first or second generations, and both were making related products during the last quarter of the century." Moreover, both companies suffered painful setbacks during the eighties. One of the main buildings of the Wakefield Rattan Company burned to the ground in 1881 and had to be completely rebuilt, and in 1888 Cyrus Wakefield II died, leaving the management of his company to relatively inexperienced men who had been in the organization with him but had little practical experience in running a business. In 1882 Heywood Brothers and Company suffered the loss of its founder, Levi Heywood, and Henry Heywood (Levi's nephew) was chosen to carry on the business. Yet both companies survived these setbacks and continued their industrial rivalry. Again, in the same commemorative speech, Greenwood told an amusing story that illustrated this rivalry between the two firms around 1883:

> Both wanted a Chicago plant and warehouse. In spite of their competing interests, they decided to establish a joint manufacturing enterprise there. Representatives of both firms met in Chicago for the purpose of finding a suitable building. The first day's search was fruitless, so it was decided to renew the quest the following day. The next morning, however, the Wakefield men left early, found a plant and informed the Heywood representatives that the building was so satisfactory that they would purchase it independently and operate it themselves. After the resulting storm subsided, Henry Heywood and Amos Morrill of Heywood Brothers and Company found a plant to their liking, which was to be the Chicago factory and warehouse until 1930. It is safe to assume that competition was keener than ever during the years following this Chicago episode.

WORKS AT WAKEFIELD.

WAKEFIELD RATTAN CO.

Importers of Rattan and Manufacturers of Rattan and Reed Furniture ; Cane and Wood Seat Chairs ; Children's Carriages ; Chair Cane ; Car Seats, etc., etc.

SALESROOMS :--Boston, New York, Chicago, San Francisco. ✳✳ FACTORIES :--Wakefield, Chicago, Kankakee, Ill., San Francisco.

After the fire of 1881, the main building of the Wakefield Rattan Company was rebuilt with brick. This print shows the Wakefield plant in the early 1890s.

Among the interesting designs in children's wicker shown here are potty chairs, rockers, and an armchair (right).

High-backed rocking chair with circular hand-caned back panel outlined with curlicues.

On March 17, 1897, under the front-page headline "Two Large Firms to Merge: An Important Consolidation to Be Made in Boston," the *New York Times* reported: "The Wakefield Rattan Company will be merged with the firm of Heywood Brothers and Company, thus effecting one of the most important consolidations of capital yet made in New England."

Less than a month later the two wicker titans formally incorporated. The newly formed company was destined to all but monopolize sales of quality wicker furniture for the next two decades. Henry Heywood, the first president of Heywood Brothers and Wakefield Company, realized the vastness of his responsibilities and rose to the challenge. Seeing the consolidation of the two great companies as a pooling of resources, he immediately began to employ Wakefield's cane-weaving machinery to produce cane seat coverings for electric streetcars as well as entire railroad seats. Of course, the main interest of the new company was still the manufacture of wicker furniture, and one of Henry Heywood's first acts as president was to establish warehouses in London and Liverpool, England, thereby creating an export market and expanding the total number of warehouses to eleven. This—coupled with the fact that the new company had huge factories in Gardner and Wakefield, Massachusetts, as well as in Chicago and San Francisco—discouraged serious competition.

The Heywood Brothers and Wakefield companies' consolidation was just in time to bid farewell to the golden age of Wicker before the twentieth century arrived with revolutionary wicker designs. While wicker furniture was still very popular in turn-of-the-century America, . the winds of change were beginning to gust.

Here are selected illustrations from the 1899 Heywood Brothers and Wakefield Company catalog, the second joint catalog put out by the newly formed company.

6266
CHILD'S CABINET CHAIR.

6267
CHILD'S CABINET CHAIR.

6268
CHILD'S CABINET CHAIR.

6269
CHILD'S CABINET CHAIR.

6279
CHILD'S CHAIR.

6280
CHILD'S ROCKING CHAIR.

2602
CHILD'S ROCKING CHAIR.

6288
CHILD'S ROCKING CHAIR.

3312
CHILD'S COMFORT ROCKING CHAIR.

6315 B. P. R.
LADY'S COMFORT PATENT ROCKER.
Fancy Colored Reeds.

6317 B. P. R.
LADY'S COMFORT PATENT ROCKER.

6315 D. P. R.
LARGE COMFORT PATENT ROCKER.
Fancy Colored Reeds.

6317 D. P. R.
LARGE COMFORT PATENT ROCKER.

*Various styles of platform rockers. All four of the examples shown here
have hollow serpentine arms and backs.*

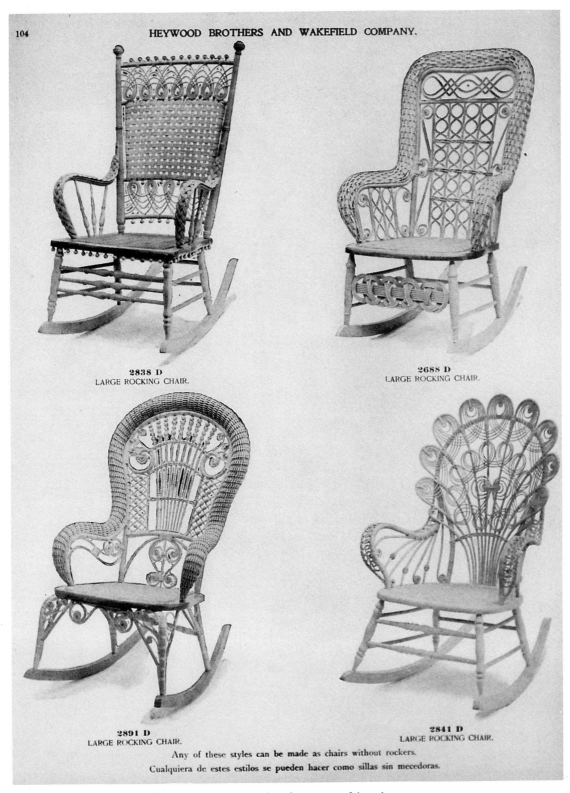

2838 D
LARGE ROCKING CHAIR.

2688 D
LARGE ROCKING CHAIR.

2891 D
LARGE ROCKING CHAIR.

2841 D
LARGE ROCKING CHAIR.

Any of these styles can be made as chairs without rockers.

Cualquiera de estos estilos se pueden hacer como sillas sin mecedoras.

Four rockers of vastly different design, yet they have one thing in common: caned seats.

6264

BEACH CHAIR.

66 inches High.

6445

DRESSING STAND.

Top, 18 x 29 Inches.

6444

FANCY CABINET.

28 x 60 Inches.

HEYWOOD BROTHERS AND WAKEFIELD COMPANY.

6259

CONVERSATION CHAIR.

6262

CONVERSATION CHAIR.

A mixed group of wicker furniture. A relative of the sixteenth-century French guérite hooded wicker chair, this 1899 version has a caned seat and side windows. Elaborate dressing stand complete with beveled mirror. Cabinet with five shelves. Two styles of the popular conversation chair. These chairs became the love seats of the Victorian era because a respectable couple could sit next to each other without touching.

*Six complete sets of matching
wicker furniture.*

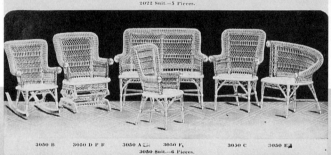

1300 B   1300 D P R   1300 F   1300 A   1300 C   1300 E
1300 Suit.—6 Pieces.

2022 A   2022 D P R   2022 F   2022 C   2022 B
2022 Suit.—5 Pieces.

*Extremely ornate bookcase and
three wicker easels, all rare pieces
of the sort eagerly sought by the
collector.*

3050 B   3050 D P R   3050 A   3050 F   3050 C   3050 E
3050 Suit.—6 Pieces.

160

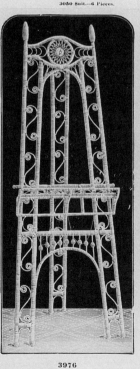

889
BOOK CASE.

891
EASEL.

3976
EASEL.
76 inches High.

894
EASEL.
72 inches High.

HEYWOOD BROTHERS AND WAKEFIELD COMPANY.

3710 E   3710 C   3710 F   3710 A   3710 D P R   3710 B
3710 Suit.—6 Pieces.

4170 B, K D   4170 C, K D   4170 F, K D   4170 D, K D   4170 A, K D
4170 K D Suit.—5 Pieces.

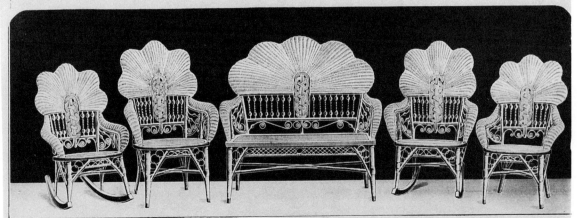

4169 B, K D   4169 C, K D   4169 F, K D   4169 D, K D   4169 A, K D
4169 K D Suit.—5 Pieces.

A PORTFOLIO OF VICTORIAN WICKER FURNITURE

1870–1900

Picture frame with rolled edges from the 1890s.

Two rockers with unique back panels. This one-of-a-kind rocker (left) is a true museum piece. The leather cameo panel set into the back is framed by wicker braiding. A gentleman's rocker (below) with a pressed-oak back panel and oak spools.

Ornate sewing basket from the 1880s.

Various styles of Victorian rock-ers. Natural serpentine rocker (above right). Lady's rocker with spider-web caning in the back (right). High-backed rocker (above). Gentleman's rocker with wooden beadwork and serpentine arms and back (far right).

A rare find: A three-piece set of natural wicker in mint condition. Both settee and matching armchairs have open horseshoe designs worked into their tightly woven backs.

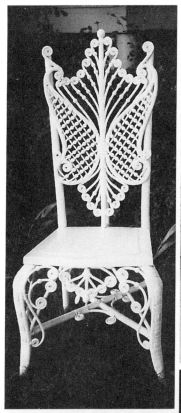

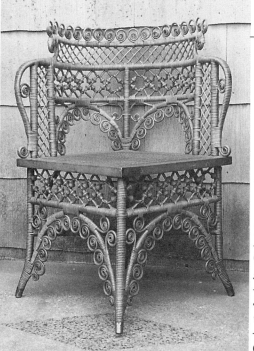

Three types of Victorian chairs.

Corner chair with elaborate use of spools and curlicues (left).

Side chair with butterfly design worked into the back (far left).

Conversation chair (below).

Side chair.

Armchair with Japanese fan
design worked into the back.

This heart-shaped Victorian design is one of the most widely
reproduced wicker designs of
modern times.

Platform rocker from the 1890s (left).

Gentleman's rocker with caned seat (far left).

Natural rocker with ornate beadwork and curlicues in the back (above left).

Serpentine rocker (above).

Lady's reception chair.

Posing chair literally dripping with curlicues.

Pie caddy.

The three fancy reception chairs shown here are typical of those used as props in most photography studios of the late 1800s. Large reception chairs like this one (above) were sometimes called bustle benches. Note the heart-shaped back.

Victorian wicker settees. Serpentine settee with spider-web caning set into the back (right).

Settee with fancywork back and caned seat (below).

Tables from the Victorian era.

Natural table with inlaid wood top and rolled sides.

Large table with birdcage design in center.

Large square table with cane-matted top and 104 curlicues.

Graceful bedside table.

Small table with extra shelf.

Three types of wicker music stands. Elaborate music stand (left) with three oak shelves. Classic music stand (top) from the 1880s. Small openwork music stand (above) with pineapple feet.

Three styles of sewing baskets, all from around 1880.

Small bric-a-brac stand with three oak shelves.

Rare organ stool with serpentine back and birdcage legs.

Rare wicker wheelchair, or phaeton.

Child's stroller with adjustable footrest.

High chair.

Extremely ornate swinging crib with canopy brace.

Baby carriage from the 1880s with parasol and wire wheels.

*Turkish bench with rolled arms
and closely woven reed seat.*

*Turkish bench with unusually
deep seat.*

*Turkish bench with diamond
design woven into seat.*

Turkish bench.

Umbrella rack.

Ornate fire screen in an
elaborate peacock design.

Circular fire screen with Dutch
windmill motif.

Square fire screen with eight
plied reed legs and finials.

Armchair with unusually high arms, scalloped reedwork, and ram's horn design at top of backrest.

Classic Victorian gentleman's armchair design.

———————————————

Armchair with snowflake-caned heart motif set into back panel (left).

Armchair with flat, rolling arms and back.

Child's rocker with star pattern woven into back panel.

Armchair employing curlicues and wooden beadwork.

Armchair with rolled arms and back made by the Whitney Reed Company.

Unique angular design frames this 1890s armchair with scalloped reed fancywork and elaborate use of wooden beadwork.

Armchair employing several weaving patterns and a gracefully slanted backrest.

Late 1890s armchair with diamond design woven into the backrest and skirting.

Armchair from the 1880s with hand-caned snowflake back panel and loop design throughout.

Elaborate gentleman's rocker (right) with beadwork woven into the center of its serpentine arms and back.

Armchair with curlicue scroll-work set into circular open back panel.

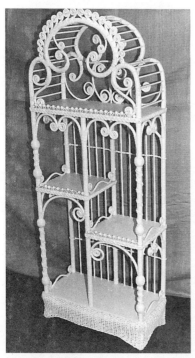

Fancy cabinet with seven shelves, stick-and-ball work, and birdcage design.

Bric-a-brac stand (above left) employing birdcage design and plied reed ball design at top. Fancy cabinet (left) with curlicues and wooden beadwork topping off loop pattern at front of shelves.

Unusual rocker with ram's horn arms, beadwork, and circular woven seat.

Rocker with cornucopia design flowing down from rolled back.

Peacock rocker (left) made by Heywood Brothers and Company in the 1880s.

Rocker with Japanese fan motif (right), unusual because it is woven from reed rather than hand caned. Also note quarter moon and star designs on either side of the fan.

Rocker with anchor motif set into backrest (below).

Very rare rocker with an American flag motif and the date 1776 set into the backrest, probably made to commemorate the centennial in 1876.

Gentleman's rocker from the 1880s.

1880s rocker with parasol motif (below left) set into hand-caned back panel.

Rocker (below) with crisscross pattern under serpentine arms and back.

Child's rocker with extensive use of wooden beadwork.

Rocker with scalloped reed pattern woven into the backrest.

Rocker with wooden beadwork (right) forming a diamond pattern in the backrest.

Child's serpentine rocker (below right) with wooden beadwork.

Gentleman's rocker (below) with unusually wide seat and rosette arm tips.

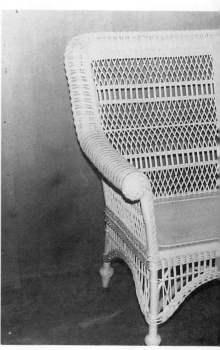

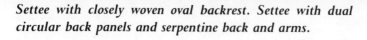

Settee with closely woven oval backrest. Settee with dual circular back panels and serpentine back and arms.

Settee with rolled arms and back. Double back settee with rolled edges.

Settee with oval hand-caned backrest and unusual serpentine back employing wooden beadwork. Settee with a circular flower motif and closely woven, arched skirting covering legs.

High chair with guitar motif set into backrest.

Doll stroller with adjustable back and parasol.

High chair with tray/footrest that locks into place.

Ornate doll buggy with heart motif and fancy turned wood finials.

Doll buggy with serpentine sides topped by curlicues.

Very rare doll buggy in the shape of a shoe with a wooden heel and crisscross "laces" up the front. Possibly a custom-made piece.

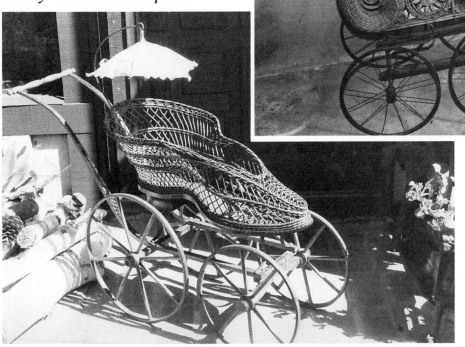

Sewing basket from the late 1890s.

Sewing basket with scallop design outlining wooden beadwork.

Sewing basket with cabriole legs and beadwork.

1890s sewing basket with original light blue paint and gilded beadwork.

Sewing basket with loop design and hand-caned top and bottom shelves.

Oblong table with scalloped reed fancywork and birdcage legs.

Round end table with wooden beadwork.

Small table with marble top.

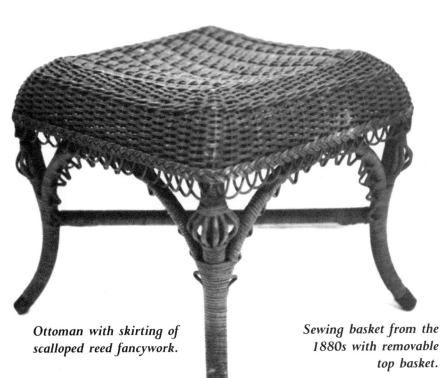

Ottoman with skirting of scalloped reed fancywork.

Sewing basket from the 1880s with removable top basket.

Umbrella stand with wooden beadwork from the late 1890s.

Ottoman with closely woven reed seat and rosette design finishing off each end.

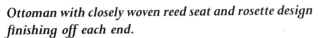

End table with stick-
and-ball work and
turned wood bead-
work on bottom
shelf.

Round end table with bottom
shelf.

Round table with serpentine legs.

Square table with cane
matting on top and
bottom shelves.

Round end table with bottom shelf.

End table with square top and diamond-shaped bottom shelf.

Square table with unique use of wooden beadwork outlining top and three shelves.

Square end table with round bottom shelf and birdcage designs.

Square table with mahogany top and plied reed fancywork.

This square table from the 1880s combines curlicues, wooden beadwork, scrollwork, and birdcage designs.

Square table with set-in caned top (above). Oblong table from the 1880s (left).

Oblong table from the 1890s (left). Square table with flowing legs (below).

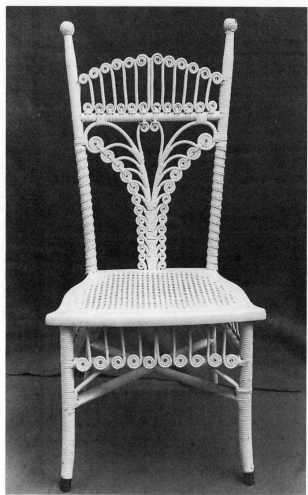

Side chair with fine braidwork wrapping posts.

Side chair with intricate fancy-work, which includes wooden beadwork incorporated into the birdcage designs on each post (right).

Side chair with fan motif in backrest.

Side chair with closely woven circular backrest.

Side chair from the 1890s made by the Whitney Reed Chair Company.

Side chair with fleur-de-lis backrest.

Side chair with serpentine back.

Side chair with heart-shaped motif in backrest.

Divan with serpentine back and wooden beadwork in backrest.

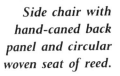

Side chair with hand-caned back panel and circular woven seat of reed.

Side chair (left) with curlicue backrest.

Fancy reception chair (far left) with flower motif and birdcage design on posts.

Lady's armchair from the late 1890s.

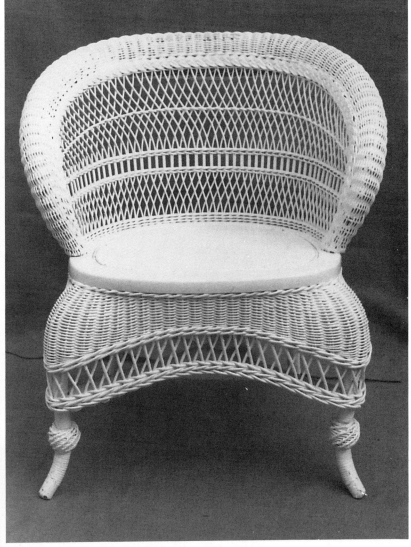

Large standing crib with rolled edges, curlicues, and wooden beadwork.

Side chair and umbrella stand in the rare cattail design.

Platform rocker in the cattail design.

Settee in the cattail design.

Divan with serpentine back and arms.

Fancy easel from the 1890s.

An 1880s easel using horizontal birdcage designs at bottom.

Lady's armchair silhouetted with curlicues.

Secretary from the 1890s with stick-and-ball work and curlicues.

Four-drawer music cabinet from the 1890s.

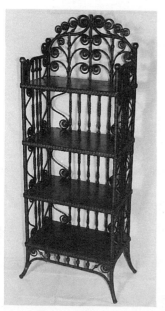

Fancy cabinet with curlicues and turned wood spindles.

Fancy cabinet with stick-and-ball work.

Fancy cabinet employing bird-cage designs, stick-and-ball work, and curlicues.

Fancy reception chair, or photographer's chair, from the 1880s.

Chaise longue with hand-caned back panel and rolled arms, back, and footrest.

Upholstered chaise longue from the 1890s.

Piano chair with swivel seat and birdcage
design on posts.

Music cabinet with lyre
motif on door and musical
notes on side.

Rare washstand with contrasting black and natural cane
woven throughout, full top
drawer and bottom cabinet.

An 1890s Heywood Brothers & Company rocking chair with sailboat motif woven into the back panel.

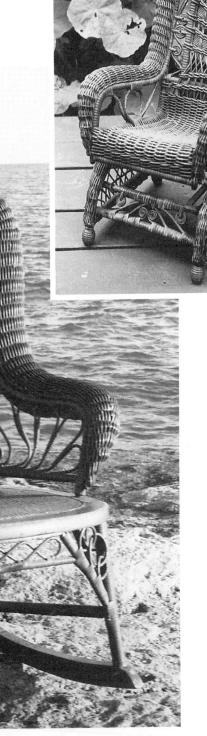

Extremely rare salesman's sample platform rocker (17 inches high).

Music stand with plied reed finials
and ball feet.

Music stand with lyre motif on top rack.

Music stand with birdcage design
and Aladdin's slipper legs.

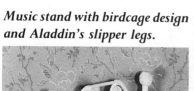

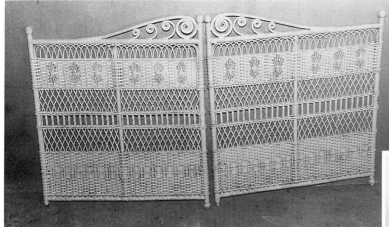

Swinging doors from the 1880s.

Fire screen from the 1880s.

**Swinging doors with
round beveled mirrors,
curlicues, and scalloped
reed fancywork.**

Music stand with wooden bead-work and turned finials.

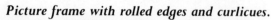
Picture frame with rolled edges and curlicues.

Music stand with oversized wooden finials.

Picture frame from the 1890s.

Platform rocker with serpentine back and arms.

Rare vanity with three oak shelves, from the 1880s.

Rocking chair embellished with curlicues and loop designs.

4

THE TURN OF THE CENTURY

Around the turn of the century a number of great changes occurred. The way people made their living was undergoing a major shift, away from agriculture and toward the rapidly growing world of trade and transportation. Not only did the automobile take the place of the horse car, but the home use of electricity and central heating became widespread, the latter of these improvements having a direct effect on the wicker furniture industry. Porches all over the country that had utilized wicker in summer were now being glassed in and warmed with the new hot-air heating system. Beyond this, sun-rooms and family rooms were also being built at a rapid rate; these rooms had an outdoor feeling while at the same time offering all the modern comforts. Wicker became "the" furniture to use in these outdoor rooms, as they were sometimes called.

According to the Wakefield Historical Society, the labor force at Heywood Brothers and Wakefield Company changed radically after 1900: many of the rattan factory workers were now of Italian extraction. The reason behind this shift from Irish to Italian workers was twofold. First, as a result of the poor economic conditions in Italy, many Italian men came to the Wakefield area to do construction work. When the projects were completed, some of the men found jobs in the rattan

Table lamp with pagoda-style shade made by Heywood Brothers and Wakefield Company.

A typical "outdoor" room furnished with wicker.

factory and then sent for their families. Second, by the early 1900s many of the next-generation Irish, whose parents and grandparents had worked for the Wakefield Rattan Company since its inception in the mid-1840s, had found different occupations, so there were many employment openings at Heywood Brothers and Wakefield Company.

From the standpoint of design, American wicker furniture of the early 1900s relied heavily on past Victorian styles, with very little experimentation. A limited number of turn-of-the-century designs had been subtly adapted to the onslaught of the Art Nouveau style, a school of design which felt that the lines occurring in nature must be the purest and therefore the most beautiful. However, true Art Nouveau wicker was a short-lived phenomenon, simply because it was designed to look as if it were growing out of the floor and therefore closely resembled many of its flowing Victorian predecessors.

Oval table with wooden bead-work in skirting.

Unfortunately, the 1900s also brought about a formidable public revolt against Victorian-style wicker furniture. Rejecting the majority of Victorian and Art Nouveau designs by 1910, Americans sought straight lines and practical styles; overly fancy wicker was suddenly considered gauche and relegated to the attic. The American consumer, for the first time since Cyrus Wakefield had begun his experiments in the 1840s, actively sought wicker furniture made outside of the United States, because foreign imports offered wicker furniture in angular rather than flowing designs.

The public discontent with the Victorian style in general first manifested itself in the increased importations of wicker furniture from the Far East. The hourglass chair from Canton (which had become marginally popular in America after the Philadelphia Centennial Exhibition of 1876) became known as the Canton chair, and before long the Chinese were exporting complete matching sets in what was generally known as the hourglass design. A. A. Vantine and Company of New York had imported this furniture direct from Canton since 1900, and their advertisements boasted of its graceful design and inexpensiveness, as well as pointing out that each piece was "woven by hand, without a nail in [its] entire construction." This Oriental wicker was lighter than its American counterpart, because the framework was made of bamboo rather than wood. Reed and rattan were woven over the bamboo frame, and in most cases the chairs had canework backs and seats.

In Europe in the late 1890s some leading members of the avant-garde Secession group in Vienna, Austria, turned their talents to designing stylized geometric wicker furniture. Designers Hans Vollmer and Gustave Funke teamed with architects Josef Hoffmann and Leopold Bauer and painter Koloman Moser to create conservative, straight-lined wicker furniture made of willow and often employing cushions and plush upholstery. In their use of overstuffed seats and upholstery many of these architect-designers seemed to disregard the basic principle on which wicker furniture had first been constructed thousands of years earlier—that woven furniture holds much the same qualities of intimacy and charm as a piece of basketry in that it is woven in the same way and shares the same spring and flexibility! And even the unupholstered angular designs seemed far more rigid because of the wide, flat seats, and therefore stood in direct contrast to most Victorian wicker furniture, which utilized slightly concave seats and backs in order to better fit the human body and give when in use. However, the American public became fascinated with the new sedate look and loved the cushioned seats and innovative fabric designs. By the early 1900s sales of imported Austrian-made wicker from such firms as Prag-Rudmiker and Ludwig Sild had skyrocketed in America, while Victorian pieces continued their drastic decline in popularity.

Austrian wicker of this period was grown in a special plot of land in the famous Vienna Prater entirely given up to the culture of different species of the willow. The wicker furniture made of these peeled osiers was an ivory white that gradually, through the years, turned a soft golden tone.

In turn-of-the-century Germany most wicker furniture manufacturers employed a professional designer or architect in order to raise the design standards of their products. In 1907 three such designers—Henry Van de Velde, Peter Behrens, and Richard Riemerschmid—joined forces to form the Deutsche Werkbund, an organization that brought designers, manufacturers, retailers, and government officials

Child's sewing basket, 26 inches high.

A turn-of-the-century Austrian design shows the rigidity of the flat, unyielding seat as opposed to earlier Victorian designs that stressed flexibility. However, the slanted backrest on this particular chair is a unique feature in wicker furniture and does give the appearance of having a somewhat elastic quality.

An Austrian-made upholstered
wicker armchair from the early
1900s. The angular construction
marked a return to basic design
as well as a revolt against the
overly ornate Victorian wicker designs still being produced in
America.

"Dryad" English Cane Furniture

THIS delightful and practical style of Summer Furniture is new to America, but is widely identified with country home life in England to-day. It finds its highest expression in the attractive and graceful Cane Chairs, Settees, Tables, Tea Waggons, Flower Stands, Dog Baskets, etc., displayed in our Division of Furniture and Decoration.

"DRYAD" Cane Furniture is without equal for use on porches and lawns. It possesses also the artistic character, substantial construction and comfortable qualities, which adapt it as well to year-round use indoors.

"DRYAD" Cane Furniture is made of the strongest unbleached pulp cane without the use of nails or tacks. The frames are of best quality ash. This construction is vastly superior to that usually found in ordinary willow, reed and rattan furniture.

The smooth finish and skillful shaping of the different models provide comfort without the necessity of cushions.

Imported and sold exclusively by us in New York and vicinity. The genuine identified by this metal label;

Illustrated Catalogue "The 'DRYAD' Cane Book" will be mailed upon request

W. & J. SLOANE

Interior Decorators   Furniture Makers

Floor Coverings and Fabrics

FIFTH AVENUE AND FORTY-SEVENTH STREET, NEW YORK

together to develop new designs and improve the quality of goods made by hand in order to better compete in international markets. The larger German firms that imported wicker furniture into America in the early 1900s included Julius Moser of Munich, Derichs + Saverteig of Coburg, and Theodor Reimann of Dresden.

While wicker furniture was also imported on a limited basis from Holland, Belgium, Switzerland, and France ("French enameled cane," a technique of interweaving strands of orange, black, and royal blue cane into chair backs, became a very popular ornamental touch during this period and can still be seen in abundance in Parisian cafés), it was England that provided the strongest competition to the Austrian and German wicker firms. The English wicker of this period, called "cane furniture" by the British, was made from willows grown in Somerset and the Thames Valley. Experiments carried out at the Leicester School of Art by headmaster Benjamin Fletcher and the most skilled basket-maker in the region, Charles Crampton, culminated in the birth of the Dryad Works in 1907. Harry Peach, Fletcher's close friend and a former bookseller, founded the firm and named it after Keats's "Ode to a Nightingale," in which the dryad, or wood nymph, is mentioned. Strongly influenced by Austrian and German designs after visiting several firms in these countries in 1906, both Fletcher and Peach felt that their wicker designs should show a greater sensitivity to such a pliant material as willow. Their aim was to produce less rigid-looking furniture by subtly shaping the framework, which, when woven with the elastic qualities of willow, would render the use of upholstery or cushions unnecessary.

By 1910 the modestly curving, circular designs offered by Dryad were immensely successful in America. Their rounded backs and full-length skirting captured a wide import business, which included W. & J. Sloane of New York. According to Dr. Pat Kirkham, the leading authority on European wicker furniture and principal lecturer at the Leicester Polytechnic School of Art History, by 1914 nearly two hundred men were employed at the Dryad Works and the demand for their wicker was so high that it obtained retail outlets in New York and Chicago. American furniture buyers were fascinated by Dryad's advertising claims that its wicker furniture was "made of the strongest unbleached pulp cane without the use of nails or tacks" and impressed with its sturdy ash framework. Well known as the exclusive importers

A 1914 magazine advertisement for Dryad English cane furniture (left).

Hanging wicker lamp.

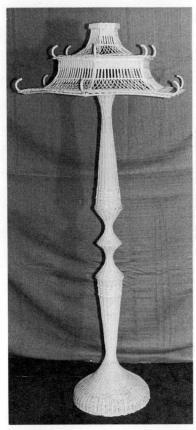

An elaborate pagoda lamp from 1915.

of this wicker, the company did a brisk mail-order business by offering an illustrated catalog, "The Dryad Cane Book," free of charge upon request.

Other English firms in Leicestershire included Ellmore (established in the 1890s) and Angraves (established in 1912), both based in Thurmanston. In 1908, a year after the establishment of Dryad, Charles Crampton's brother, Albert, defected from Dryad to establish his own firm, Casdons, at nearby Castle Donnington. Sadly, Albert Crampton not only felt free to blatantly copy Dryad designs, he also plagiarized product names and the entire layout of Dryad's leaflets and trade catalogs.

In America the art of woven furniture survived because of its inherent adaptability, but it took wicker manufacturers several years to realize that they would have to change with the times or lose their market. Although some Victorian designs were still lingering in 1915, they were forced to share the spotlight with the new and sobering influence of the angular, straight-lined styles as can be seen in two pages from the Sears, Roebuck and Company catalog of 1915.

Oddly, it wasn't one of the well-known wicker firms that finally began producing sedate, angular wicker furniture in this country, but rather the Gustav Stickley Company in Eastwood, New York, established in 1898. Stickley's main interest was in designing oak furniture in the Mission style (sometimes called "Craftsman" furniture). However, in the early 1900s Stickley began designing some straight-lined, no-nonsense wicker made of willow, and the public loved it. Although Stickley's wicker designs were influenced by earlier Austrian designs and Shaker furniture, his Mission-style wicker had a look and feel of its own. Here was America's answer to the flood of Austrian and English imports.

Eventually the owners of the newly formed Heywood Brothers and Wakefield Company realized that the Mission style was here to stay, and by 1905 they had begun producing similar designs to conform to current tastes. Around this time practical adaptations also began to appear in greater numbers—added touches such as circular refresh-

A Victorian side chair with a lyre motif set into the back panel and an elaborate 1880s side chair with extensive use of curlicues and wooden beadwork.

In the 1880s the so-called peacock design became a favorite with the public. Here a matching armchair, table, and platform rocker display the symmetry that won this design favor.

The detail work on this 1890s side chair (right) is emphasized by fancy colored reeds and wooden beadwork.

An unusually stylish phonograph cabinet (below) from the turn of the century. Many wicker phonographs were designed to play flat disc records; this extremely rare example predates these models and plays cylinders.

This mid-Victorian corner whatnot (above) is one of the rarest pieces of wicker in the country. The elaborate fancywork and triangular design can be deceptive—the piece is a full seven feet in height.

A Victorian armchair (left) with a hand-caned cameo-shaped back panel and a vertically woven reed seat.

This Victorian oblong table utilizes green-stained wooden beadwork to enhance the design.

The graceful shell design is employed in this natural wicker square table and flanking side chairs (above).

This child's rocker (left) from the 1880s has the popular heart-shaped motif set into its back panel.

The flowing, octopuslike lines of this 1890s round table (below) is outlined with curlicues and scrollwork.

Clockwise: This late-Victorian armchair employs figure-eight fancywork woven into the closely woven backrest and skirting. A platform rocker from the 1880s period. This particular design employs the Japanese fan motif woven into the back panel. The backrest of this turn-of-the-century Morris chair is adjustable to four positions. Fancy reception chairs like this 1890s example were also known as photographer's chairs, due to their frequent use as props in Victorian portrait studios.

Revolving four-tier bookcase from the late-Victorian era.

This late-Victorian divan (above) is silhouetted by a graceful serpentine back and armrest. The lower back combines wooden beadwork with closely woven reed.

This desk set (left) was handmade of fiber in the early twenties. The design is highlighted by the use of colored staining.

Wicker tea carts were popular after 1910. This early twenties example (left) has a lift-off glass tray and three shelves. The green stain is original from the factory.

An 1880s gentleman's armchair (far left) with snowflake-caned lower back panel.

An 1890s armchair with fancy colored reeds and an oval back panel.

This 1890s rocker has a serpentine back and arms as well as a rare leather cameo panel set into the backrest.

Late-Victorian armchair with rolled arms, birdcage legs, and liberal use of curlicues.

This Victorian armchair does double duty; it converts into a Turkish bench by removing the backrest, which is secured by two metal rods and eyelets attached to the back of the frame.

This tripod end table (far left) employs a clover-shaped top and the generous use of wooden bead-work. This small bric-a-brac stand (left) is 45 inches high and makes use of four oak tiers.

Matching armchair, table, and chaise longue from the World War I era. Note that one arm of the chaise is lower than the other, intended as the side for easy entrance.

This square table (left) from the 1890s makes use of plied reeds to cover the bottom third of its legs, vertical braces, and finials.

This matching table and divan (below) from the 1890s is dominated by flowing, leaflike designs that are outlined with fancy colored reeds.

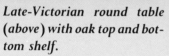

Late-Victorian round table (above) with oak top and bottom shelf.

An 1880s rocker (below) with hand-caned backrest and a unique curved headrest in the intricate snowflake pattern.

This 1880s armchair (left) is a good example of the "fancy colored reeds" popular during the Victorian era. The design itself makes use of unconventional armrests and funnel-shaped stick-and-ball fancywork on the front legs.

ment holders built into the arms of chairs and lounges, retractable footrests on armchairs, and woven side pockets under the armrests of rockers and chairs, which were used as handy receptacles for magazines and knitting supplies. The Heywood Brothers and Wakefield Company had adapted to the times and business was booming again. In 1913 their Chicago plant had to be enlarged, and in 1916 they purchased the outstanding stock of the Washburn and Heywood Chair Company. Beyond this, the company continued in their longtime tradition of supplying seats for streetcars and railroads.

A Mission-style armchair from 1910.

Reed Furniture

Popular Reed Rocker

Only

$2.99

This is the most popular Reed Rocker we have ever sold. It is made of imported reeds, finished in shellac over a thoroughly seasoned frame of maple, doweled and glued, insuring a very rigid and substantial rocker. Has a wide, roomy seat, comfortable roll arms and high back, together with a perfect rest giving quality not usually found in other rockers at a much higher price. Shipping weight, about 14 pounds.

No. 1D910

Price,

$2.99

Because of the rounding curved lines, and the suppleness and flexibility of the reeds, reed furniture is exceptionally comfortable. Another reason for its popularity is its lightness, making it very easy to handle and move about. There is a great difference in the various makes of reed furniture, and extreme care should be taken in its selection. All our rockers and settees are made of an excellent quality of imported reeds. The frames are carefully constructed of seasoned Northern hardwood and are made of stock of ample size to insure perfect strength. The posts and cross stretchers are carefully fitted, securely fastened, making a solid, strong and rigid piece. The imported reeds are tough, flexible fibers, and will not break or split. They are closely woven by hand by highly skilled workmen. The finish is very carefully applied and is very durable.

NO HOME is complete without at least one or two reed rockers, and you will find a very wide selection on this and the next page. We make you a big saving in price because of our direct method of merchandising. You do not have to pay the big profits of a long chain of jobbers, dealers, retailers, etc., when you buy from us. Buying in enormous quantities to supply our many thousands of customers, we are able to secure from the manufacturers the lowest possible prices. These benefits are in turn given to our customers. Our prices speak for themselves. We welcome the closest comparison.

Cane Seat Reed Rocker

Only

$3.28

A choice unique design that will fit well into almost every home, no matter what the other furnishings may be. Made of an excellent quality imported reeds, shellac finish, woven over a thoroughly seasoned frame of maple. Very strong and rigid. A heavy continuous closely woven roll entirely surrounding back, arms and seat. Beneath the seat is a medium size reed skirt. The roomy, comfortable seat is covered with a fine quality of closely woven cane. Would command a much higher price elsewhere. Shipping wt., about 15 pounds.

No. 1D919

Price,

$3.28

Remarkably Good Values—Remarkably Good Rockers.

Price, **$2.43**

No. 1D903 A popular pattern at a remarkably low price. Made with flat continuous arms and closely woven back. The frame is made of thoroughly seasoned hardwood. Excellent quality reeds. Finished in natural shellac. Broad roomy seat. Roll front. Strong, rigid and durable. A splendid value. Shipping wt., about 13 pounds.

Price, **$2.68**

No. 1D905 Large Comfortable Reed Rocker, has extra high back and wide seat, closely woven with double strand reeds. Has full continuous roll around back and arms. The frame is made of thoroughly seasoned hardwood, natural shellac finish. This rocker is firmly constructed and a wonderfully good value at our low price. Shipping weight, about 12 pounds.

Price, **$3.78**

No. 1D924 This Women's Reed Rocker only $3.78. The reeds are an excellent imported stock. Extra wide back with continuous roll arms extending under seat and supported by scrolls. Wide seat covered with fine cane, and almost solid reed back. Solidly constructed frame of seasoned hardwood, natural finish. An excellent value at our low price. Shipping weight, about 17 pounds.

Price, **$3.86**

No. 1D927 Large Size Reed Rocker, one of the latest designs. Constructed with a view to comfort and durability. It has a wide roll seat, full wrapped continuous arms and posts, and is made over a maple frame, thoroughly seasoned. Carefully wrapped and packed and safe delivery guaranteed. Shipping weight, about 15 pounds.

Price, **$3.98**

No. 1D935 Handsome Cane Seat Reed Rocker, exceptionally well made. Has low back with beautiful heavy roll extending from back over the arms to seat. Frame is firmly braced underneath seat. Natural shellac finish. It is one of the most popular styles and is an exceptional value at the price we ask. Shipping weight, about 14 pounds.

Price, **$3.97**

No. 1D931 Extra Wide Back Comfortable Rocker, made of an excellent quality of imported reeds over a thoroughly seasoned hardwood frame. Wide, roomy seat. Heavy continuous roll is closely woven and extends entirely around back and arms. This is a big roomy rocker having unusual comfort giving qualities. Shipping weight, about 15 pounds.

Price, **$4.24**

No. 1D938 Combination Nurse's or Sewing Rocker. A comfortable practical rocker for women's use. Has low arm rests, medium high back and basket at the side for holding sewing material or other articles. Frame is seasoned maple, doweled and firmly glued. The reed work is all of imported stock finished golden brown. Shipping weight, about 14 pounds.

Price, **$4.68**

No. 1D941 Made of selected imported reeds over a thoroughly seasoned hardwood frame. Natural shellac finish. Large, roomy seat with roll front and a continuous roll extending over back and arms. This is a broad, spacious, restful rocker that will make any room in your home vastly more inviting and comfortable. Shipping weight, about 16 pounds.

Price, **$5.98**

No. 1D944 Large Comfortable Reed Rocker. Made of selected imported reeds over a thoroughly seasoned maple frame. Finished in natural shellac. Has wide roomy seat and high back. The heavy continuous roll is closely woven and extends entirely around the back over arms and front posts. A big, high grade rocker that will give good service. Shipping wt., about 17 lbs.

Price, **$6.18**

No. 1D947 This Rocker is built with a comfortable spring seat, padded back and has the low arms. Has extra roomy basket on side for sewing materials or other articles. The frame is made of seasoned maple. The seat is 17x19 inches. The reeds are all imported and are finished in the golden brown finish. Has beautifully figured cretonne back and seat cushions. Shipping weight, about 17 pounds.

A Complete Kitchen and Pantry Wall Cabinet Priced Very Low—See China Pages

Upholstered Reed Set for Den, Living Room and Porch

This beautiful three-piece reed set provides a strong, serviceable and sanitary furnishing for den, living room, veranda, summer-house, lawn or club house. It combines to a greater degree than any other kind of furniture the qualities of strength, utility, durability and lightness of weight. The quiet brown finish and the beautifully contrasting cretonne cushions add a tone of color and warmth to any room, sun parlor or porch. Another desirable feature of this splendid suite is that it harmonizes with various other types of furniture, lending a tone of added luxury to any furnished room.

The frame of each piece is made of thoroughly seasoned maple. The reeds are a choice imported stock and are carefully woven over the frames. The finish is a rich golden brown and is very popular for this style of furniture. Owing to its neutral tone of color it readily harmonizes with any other furnishings and the draperies in your home. This finish will not show finger marks or become soiled easily.

A special feature in the construction of this high grade reed set is the full spring seats. The rocker and chair have six springs and the settee has twelve springs, which together with the soft padded cushions and the back cushions makes each piece extremely comfortable. The cushions are covered with beautiful floral figured art pattern cretonne, in bright colors, giving the set a very inviting and cheerful appearance.

THE ROCKER—Seat, 18x20 inches; height of back from seat, 18 inches; entire height, 31 inches. Full spring seat fitted with steel cone shape springs. Loose seat cushion. Large attached cushion on top of back. Shipping weight, about 16 pounds.

THE SETTEE—Seat, 18x38 inches. Height of back from seat, 18 inches; entire height, 32½ inches. Seat has full spring construction with twelve steel cone shape springs. Seat cushion is loose and can be removed. Large attached cushion on top of back as illustrated. Metal shoes on bottom of legs. Shipping weight, about 27 pounds.

THE ARM CHAIR—Seat, 18x20 inches; height of back from seat, 18 inches; entire height, 32 inches. Seat is of full spring construction with best steel cone springs. The seat cushion is loose and can be removed. Has attached back cushion as illustrated. Metal shoes on bottom of legs. Shipping weight, about 15 pounds.

No. 1D994

Settee. Price	$12.95
Rocker. Price	6.75
Arm Chair. Price	6.65

These *Reed Rest Rockers* Are Comfortable and Cozy—Ideal for Living Room

THE FRAMES are all made of thoroughly seasoned maple, carefully doweled and firmly glued. **THE REEDS** are all selected imported stock, tough, pliable and durable.

THE FINISH is a rich, golden brown. Especially adapted in color tone and wearing qualities to this type of furniture.

$5.25

A Popular Comfortable Reed Rocker. The left arm is built in the form of a basket, making this an especially desirable rocker for the library or living room. Roomy seat, 18x19 inches. Height of back from seat, 19 inches. Entire height, 30 inches. Brown finish. Shipping wt., about 12 pounds.
No. 1D956 Price...$5.25

$7.95

A Magazine Reed Rocker of a very popular type. The pockets under each arm are convenient for papers, magazines, etc. The seat and back are fitted with beautifully figured cretonne covered cushions. Full spring seat, 20x20 inches. Height of back from seat, 23 inches. Entire height, 34 inches. Brown finish. Shipping weight, about 16 pounds.
No. 1D961 Price...$7.95

$8.25

High Arm Broad Back Reed Rocker. Broad gracefully curved arms each 5 inches wide. Back is 21 inches high from the seat. Entire height, 34 inches. Full spring seat, 20x20 inches. The seat and back are fitted with figured cretonne covered cushions in bright, cheerful color effects. Brown finish. Shipping weight, about 24 pounds.
No. 1D966 Price...$8.25

$8.75

Extra Large Reed Rocker. Made with the knockdown construction, allowing it to be shipped in a small flat package eliminating liability to damage. Richly upholstered in floral figured tapestry. Seat has the full spring construction containing six steel cone shape springs and is 20x19 in.; height of back from seat, 22 in. Entire height, 31½ inches. Shipped knocked down. Brown finish. Shipping weight, about 24 pounds.
No. 1D974 Price...$8.75

$8.45

High Back Magazine Reed Rocker with spring seat containing six steel cone shape springs. Seat has loose cushion and the back has a large attached cushion, both covered with good quality cretonne. The left arm has a deep basket for magazines, papers or other articles. Seat, 20x20 inches. Height of back from seat, 28 inches. Entire height, 40 inches. Brown finish. Shipping weight, 24 pounds.
No. 1D970 Price...$8.45

$8.95

Fireside Reed Rocker with spring seat, broad back with wings on each side. Back upholstered with beautiful figured cretonne covered cushion. The seat contains six steel cone shape springs covered with heavy duck. Loose seat cushion covered with cretonne to match back. Seat, 18x20 inches; height of back from seat, 23 inches; entire height, 35 inches. Brown finish. Shipping wt., 21 pounds.
No. 1D977 Price...$8.95

$9.45

English Fireside Reed Rocker with broad high cushioned back and large spring seat. The left arm has deep basket for papers, magazines, pipe and tobacco or other articles. The seat is made with six steel cone shape springs and is 19½x20 in. Height of back from seat, 26 in. Entire height, 42 in. Back and seat fitted with beautifully figured cretonne covered cushions. Brown finish. Shipping weight, 23 pounds.
No. 1D981 Price...$9.45

$10.95

Our Finest Reed Rocker. A big, lounging design, solid comfort rocker. Extra high curved form fitting back, 30 inches high from seat to top, fitted with tufted cretonne covered cushion and head roll at top. Entire height, 40 inches. Full spring seat with six steel cone shape springs. It is 20½x22½ inches and has a beautifully figured cretonne covered cushion to match the back. Broad, rounding arms. Brown finish. Shipping weight, about 26 pounds.
No. 1D985 Price...$10.95

'All Well Fed and Happy"—The Story Our Grocery Catalog Carries to a Million Homes.

SEARS, ROEBUCK AND CO., CHICAGO, ILL. **1089**

This 1908 Union Pacific Railroad dome car utilizes cane seating stuffed with horsehair. The loom on which these seats were woven was invented in 1870 by William Houston, an employee of the Wakefield Rattan Company.

Mission-style armchair with magazine rack woven into the outside of the right arm and umbrella holder woven into the outside of the left arm.

Fernery with fancy gesso flowers winding up the base.

While wicker baby carriages underwent significant changes during this period, they never suffered the drastic dip in popularity other forms of wicker did during this transitional era. Turn-of-the-century parents had quite a selection: from topless "Park Carts" to large "Pullman Sleeper Coaches" complete with fancy parasols and plush interiors. The two-wheeled "Sulkies" and ever-popular "Go-Carts" (a semicollapsible design developed by the Block Go-Cart Company of Philadelphia) were the best sellers of the day. The most bizarre design in pre-1920 baby carriages was the 1916 Heywood Brothers and Wakefield Company's miniature version of a Ford automobile, complete with ball-bearing wheels, side lamps, license plate, windshield, nickel-plated hubcaps, corduroy upholstery, rubber tires, woven fenders, and two side porthole windows.

In 1915 Heywood Brothers and Wakefield Company was the sole manufacturer of "Perfek'tone" wicker phonograph cabinets. These unique phonographs were advertised as the most advanced music machines ever produced, for the handmade reed cabinets were said to

Pages from the 1919 Perfek'tone catalog of wicker phonographs.

Perfektone

The Perfek'tone Reproducer is made to match with scientific exactness the perfect construction of the human organs of sound.

The effect of the Perfek'tone Reproducer is such that even the untrained ear can appreciate the purity of tone. The elimination of all metallic and mechanical sounds means that the 'greatest barrier to the successful reproduction of sound has been overcome.

The Horn, or tone amplifier, is of special design and construction. It is composed of a matrix of wood and fabric having a peculiar vibratory action of its own, and gives a fullness and sweetness of tone which can be compared to a rare old violin. Violins made of this material reproduce the tones of very old and seasoned wood.

The Perfek'tone Cabinet is the last word in acoustical science as applied to sound-reproducing instruments, having no confined air spaces or cavities to destroy the original coloring of the music. The counter vibrations, so noticeable with wood cabinets, are entirely eliminated by the use of reed and cane.

These three things control the perfect reproduction of the music. They are contained in all Perfek'tone instruments, making the quality and tone of the music the same, irrespective of the size and shape of the cabinet.

Perfektone

STYLE No. 8, $400—OLD IVORY OR VERD MAHOGANY AND OTHER COLORS WITHOUT EXTRA CHARGE. HEAVY DUTY, TRIPLE SPRING MOTOR. ELECTRICALLY DRIVEN, $50 EXTRA. METAL PARTS GOLD, SILVER OR NICKEL-PLATED. SIZE 50 INCHES HIGH—21 INCHES WIDE—23 INCHES DEEP.

PLAYS ALL RECORDS

eliminate the annoying "countervibrations" so noticeable in conventional wood cabinets. With both floor and table models available, as well as a choice of hand-cranked and electrically driven triple-spring-motor varieties, the consumer was further tempted by specialized catalogs filled with unusual designs and graphic descriptions of these beautiful cabinets. Four pages from the 1919 Perfek'tone catalog give us a closer look at this rare wicker item, which is seldom seen today.

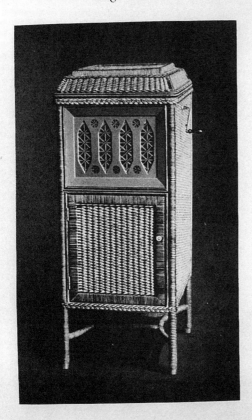

Perfektone

STYLE No. 74. $150—VERD MAHOGANY, OLD IVORY, HOLLAND GRAY OR FRENCH WALNUT AND OTHER COLORS WITHOUT EXTRA CHARGE. DOUBLE SPRING MOTOR. SIZE 48 INCHES HIGH—20¼ INCHES WIDE—23½ INCHES DEEP.

PLAYS ALL RECORDS

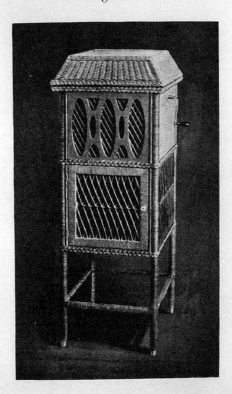

Perfektone

STYLE No. 67½. $115—VERD MAHOGANY, OLD IVORY, HOLLAND GRAY, FRENCH WALNUT AND OTHER COLORS WITHOUT EXTRA CHARGE. DOUBLE SPRING MOTOR. PLAYS FOUR 10-INCH RECORDS WITH ONE WINDING. SIZE 47 INCHES HIGH—19½ INCHES WIDE—22½ INCHES DEEP.

PLAYS ALL RECORDS

Smoking stand from 1910.

Between the turn of the century and World War I the American wicker furniture industry met the challenge of a rapidly changing world and a shift in public taste and proved to be its equal. Wicker was again riding high. It had also gained the acceptance of leading decorators such as James Collier Marshall, whose article "Among the Wicker Shops" appeared in *Country Life in America* magazine in May 1914:

> In going about among the shops one is impressed by the quantity of wicker furniture on display everywhere, and particularly by the great variety of designs and the number of different weaves . . . this indication

Tea cart with lift-off tray and glassed-in compartment.

of the rapidly growing popularity of wicker is easily accounted for by the fact that the public has come to consider it as a legitimate article of interior decoration rather than as a makeshift for porch and lawn use during the summer seasons . . . the manufacturer, anticipating this increase in favor, has evolved furniture of such excellence in design and construction as has never before been thought of in this kind of work; articles for everyday use that compel one's admiration and intrigue one's desire . . . from the decorative viewpoint, the chairs particularly rank very high since they are the one modern manufacture that harmonizes well with any type of antique furniture. Perhaps this is because wickerwork is older than history itself. Whatever the reason, a wicker chair will find an agreeable niche for itself in any setting and often proves a softening leaven in a group of forbidding looking Ancients!

Rare set of matching armchair, table, settee, and rocker, in original factory paint job of dark green with gold highlights. Handmade of fiber around 1910.

A PORTFOLIO OF WICKER FURNITURE

TURN OF THE CENTURY

Large six-sided cabinet table with scalloped reed fancywork.

Stylish settee with prominent plied reed finials.

Floor lamp with original gold and black fringe under pagoda-style shade and handy table at mid-level.

Child's rocker from 1915, handmade of fiber.

Camel-back rocker with upholstered seat and back.

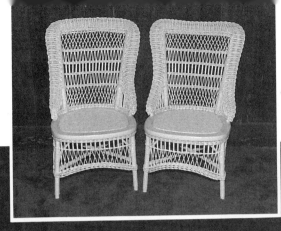

Matching set of side chairs from 1900.

Settee in the Mission style made c. 1910.

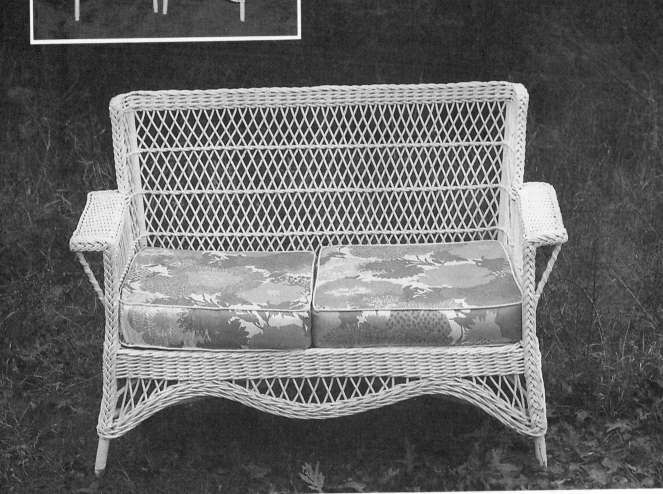

Wicker couch or daybed.

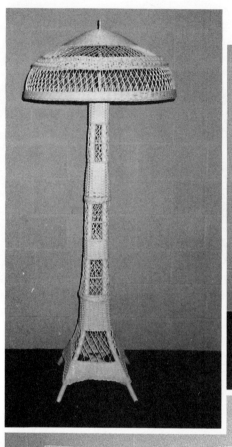

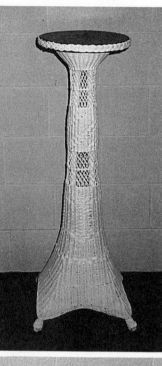

Floor lamp (far left) with "Eiffel Tower"-style base.

Round plant stand (left), c. 1910.

Sofa with window design inside diamond pattern woven into each back panel.

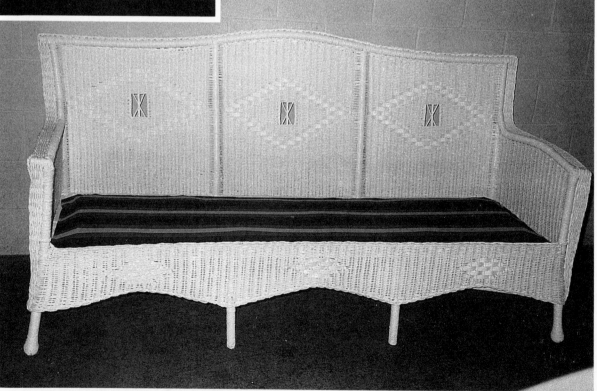

Plant stand with unique dual-level design.

A tightly woven settee.

Unique Art Nouveau double planter with bird-cage (far left).

Fernery (left) made from raffia using the cornucopia motif.

Blanket chest with hinged lid, diamond design, and scalloped reed fancywork.

Blanket chest with set-in caned top, c. 1910.

Plant stand with metal liner and turned wood framework.

Plant stand, c. 1915.

Empire-style oblong table with massive legs from the early 1900s.

Oblong table from 1915.

Oblong table from the early 1900s employing curlicue design.

Oval table with magazine pockets woven into bottom shelf.

Armchair, c. 1910.

Wing-back armchair in the Mission style, with magazine holder.

Wing-back armchair with large dual magazine pockets under arms.

Armchair with turned wood framework and reed diamond pattern woven into the framework.

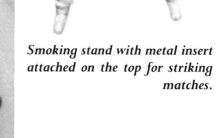

Smoking stand with metal insert attached on the top for striking matches.

Round end table exhibiting three types of braidwork.

Armchair with magazine pockets under each arm.

Rare china cabinet from 1900 with wooden beadwork woven into the top and bottom, glass-fronted cupboard, and side panels. Six feet in height.

Round table from 1900 with revolving bookcase on bottom shelf.

Three styles of wood baskets from the early 1900s.

Standing crib combining open lattice-work and closely woven skirting.

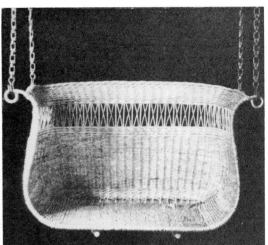

A wicker porch swing, c. 1914.

Kneeling bench from the early 1900s.

Baby buggy from 1915 with adjustable woven hood, turntable gear, and rubber tires.

Extremely rare custom-made player piano with matching bench and music cabinet for piano rolls. Wickerwork is natural and the diamond patterns are painted orange and black. The piano was made in 1906 by the Stuyvesant Piano Company of New York City. The wicker manufacturer is unknown.

Octagon-shaped dining table and chairs from 1900.

Umbrella stand with metal liner at bottom.

Octagonal dining table and chairs, c. 1910.

Sewing basket with semicircular drawer that revolves outward and two small side drawers for thread and needles.

Sewing basket with two shelves outlined with wooden beadwork.

Sewing basket with braided overlay and birdcage design on legs.

Child's sewing basket made of raffia and manufactured in Germany.

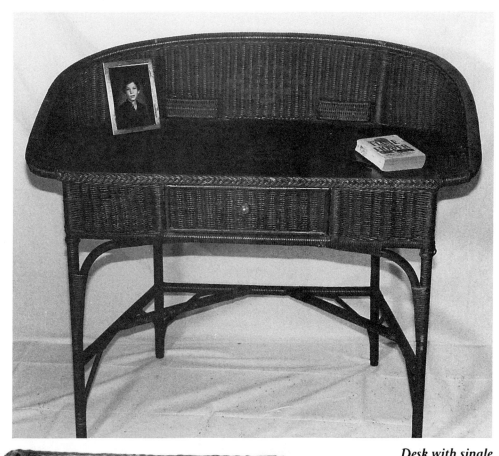

Desk with single drawer and woven letter holders from 1910.

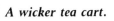

A wicker tea cart.

Four-tiered bookcase from the turn of the century.

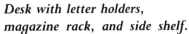

Desk with letter holders, magazine rack, and side shelf.

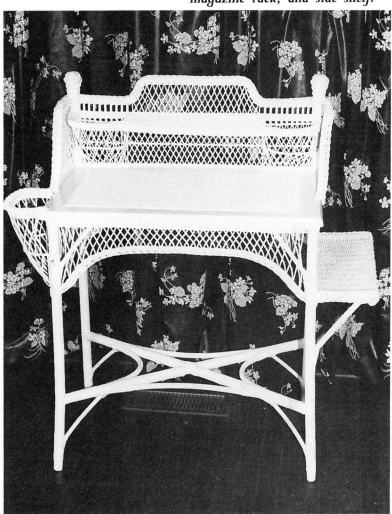

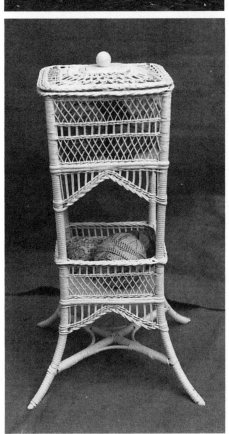

Sewing basket (left) from the early 1900s.

Desk (far left) with cubbyhole gallery top and plied reed pineapple feet.

Genuine Reed Furniture

Frames are made of maple, over which the reeds are carefully woven. The finish is a rich golden brown. Full steel coil spring construction. Rocker and chair have **nine** steel coil springs and the settee has **eighteen** steel coil springs, which together with the removable seat cushions and the attached well padded back cushions, make each piece extremely comfortable. Settee has **three** loose cushions. Cushions and backs are covered with floral figured art pattern cretonne, in bright colors. Metal shoes on bottom of rear legs of rocker.

Arm Chair—Seat, **20x20** inches. Height of back from seat, **22½** inches. Entire height, **36** inches.

Settee—Seat, **23x66** inches. Height of back from seat, **21½** inches. Entire height, **36½** inches. Entire length, **79** inches.

Rocker—Seat, **20x20** inches. Height of back from seat, **22½** inches. Entire height, **35** inches.

1N995

Settee .....(Shpg. wt., 115 lbs.)....	$44.45
Rocker ....(Shpg. wt., 28 lbs.)....	17.95
Arm Chair..(Shpg. wt., 28 lbs.)....	17.85

This Fernery with Bird Cage attached will add to the attractiveness of any home.

Genuine reed, brown finish, woven over a strong hardwood frame. Inside fitted with galvanized steel pan. Bird cage is large and roomy. Entire height, 62½ in. Size of fernery, 12x28 in. Size of cage, 11½x13½ inches. Shipping weight, 50 pounds.
1N969 ....**$17.75**

Basket portion made of reed. Supporting rods and cross-pieces made of hardwood in turned pattern. Brown finish. Inside fitted with galvanized steel pan. Height, **31** inches. Length, **28** inches. Width, **11½** inches. Shipping weight, 20 lbs.
1N967
$6.95
Price does not include the ferns.

This Reed Table is made of hardwood, over which the reed has been skillfully woven. Nicely finished in rich golden brown color. Would look very well with our 1N995 set, listed above at the left. Height, 26 inches. Top, 30 inches in diameter. Shipping weight, 20 pounds.
1N985 ....**$7.65**

A very beautiful Reed Rocker. Golden brown finish. Full steel coil construction in seat with loose spring cushion covered with floral art cretonne. Height, **36** inches. Height of back from seat, **23** inches. Seat, **19½x19** inches. Arms, **3¾** inches wide. Shipping weight, 29 pounds.
1N991 ....**$13.45**

This popular style Tea Wagon is woven of genuine reed, brown finish, over a strongly constructed hardwood frame. Has removable tray with bottom lined with cretonne. Convenient shelf at each end. Very useful, and will be an attractive addition to your dining room. Height over all, 29 inches. Size of removable tray is 14½x21½ inches. Size of wheels, 14 inches in diameter, with heavy rubber tires. Shipping weight, 40 pounds.
1N999 ....**$13.65**

26x42-Inch Top.

The fancy weaving adds greatly to the appearance of this Rocker. Golden brown finish. Loose cushion seat, nicely covered with cretonne. Height of back from seat, **20** inches. Seat, **20x20** inches. Arms, **5** inches wide. Shipping weight, 20 lbs.
1N992 ....**$14.85**

An attractive Reed Library Table. This table will match our 1N995 set, described at top of page. It is strongly constructed of hardwood, wrapped with genuine reed, golden brown finish, and has a genuine veneered quarter sawed oak top. Shipping weight, 65 pounds.
1N988 ....**$15.65**

Attractive Reed Wrapped Table Book Stand, Golden Brown Finish. Made of select reeds woven over hardwood frame. Has three hardwood book shelves and table top. Reed braid trimmed. Top, 16 inches square. Shelves, 12 inches square. Entire height, 29½ inches. Shipping weight, 20 pounds. **Shipped set up, wrapped.**
1N987 ....**$7.85**

5

THE TWENTIES

I n 1927 the Roaring Twenties hit its zenith. Duke Ellington organized a band that began a five-year stand at Harlem's Cotton Club; Babe Ruth hit sixty home runs; President Coolidge announced that he would not run for president in 1928; the Academy of Motion Picture Arts and Sciences was founded; and writer Sinclair Lewis's novel about religious charlatanism, *Elmer Gantry,* became a best seller. Flappers, bathtub gin, and the bull market. One of the most popular songs of 1927 was "Blue Skies," a timely little tune seeing that the biggest event of a big year was Charles A. Lindbergh's solo flight across the Atlantic. Taking off in the rain from Roosevelt Field, Long Island, on May 20, the young pilot refused to take a radio or other instruments in order to save weight for ninety additional gallons of gasoline. Every conceivable measure was taken to keep the weight on board to a minimum so as to take on more fuel. As it was, the aircraft was so heavily laden with 451 gallons of gasoline that it barely cleared some telephone wires on takeoff. Some thirty-three hours later the young hero landed at Le Bourget outside Paris. "Lucky Lindy" had flown the *Spirit of St. Louis* alone across the Atlantic by the seat of his pants—and the seat of his pants rested on a wicker chair, chosen both for its light weight and its comfort.

In the early 1900s wicker furniture was designed to be made with

This page (left) from the 1923 Sears, Roebuck and Company catalog clearly illustrates the popularity of upholstered wicker in the mid-twenties. G. W. Randall and Company of Michigan manufactured wicker furniture for Sears, Roebuck from 1890 through the 1920s.

A Bar Harbor wicker rocker. Manufacturers used this open-work weaving technique to cut down the cost of labor and material.

open latticework, to lessen the cost of labor. The costly, closely woven "Cape Cod" furniture gave way to cheaper open-weave willow or reed pieces that came to be known as Bar Harbor wicker, after the popular Maine resort town. Made in a wide-open pattern of latticework, the Bar Harbor design attracted a lot of attention and soon became an alternative to the strict and somewhat confining lines dictated by the Mission style. Still clean and simple of line, Bar Harbor wicker shared the spotlight with the Mission style.

The flat fabric loom (or Lloyd loom, as it came to be called) revolutionized the wicker furniture industry.

Then, in 1904, public demand for lower-priced, closely woven wicker furniture was answered with the advent of fiber, sometimes called "fiber reed" or "fiber rush." This highly pliable twisted paper was man-made, and so inexpensive that closely woven furniture could be constructed of it very reasonably. The twisted paper was treated with a glue size, which stiffened it and helped preserve the shape of the furniture. Sometimes it was wrapped around an inner core of wire at stress points in the design, to ensure durability. Perhaps the most popular feature of wicker furniture made of the new fiber material was its resistance to breakage; it would not break as readily as reed or rattan. Still, reed was used far more than fiber in the making of pre-1920 wicker furniture.

In 1906 Marshall B. Lloyd, a well-known inventor and manufacturer of handwoven reed baby buggies, moved his plant to Menominee, Michigan, and restructured his Lloyd Manufacturing Company. More than a decade later, in 1917, Lloyd invented a machine to weave wicker furniture, and this invention changed the face of the industry overnight. From earliest times wicker articles had been woven by hand, and although many nineteenth-century inventors (among them Cyrus Wakefield and Levi Heywood) had tried to invent a machine that could weave the material onto a frame, none had met with success. Marshall Lloyd finally succeeded by using his imagination to develop a totally new method of construction. This new method, whereby the material was woven on a loom and the frames were built independently, according to patterns, was at the same time simple and amazing. When both the weaving and the wooden frame were completed, the woven material was carefully fitted over the framework. Because of its great flexibility and lower cost, Lloyd used fiber as the weaving material. He quickly became one of the largest producers of wicker baby buggies in America.

Marshall B. Lloyd.

Combination fernery and birdcage.

LLOYD SHOP NEWS

PUBLISHED BY AND FOR THE EMPLOYEES OF THE LLOYD MANUFACTURING COMPANY

VOLUME 1   MENOMINEE, MICHIGAN, JULY 25, 1921   NUMBER 13

AUGUST 13 IS THE BIG PICNIC DAY

A SQUARE DEAL APPRECIATED BY LLOYD WORKERS

The Golden Rule Law Has Always Been in Action at the Lloyd Factory.

That's the general feeling among the Lloyd people. They are proud of a record that is hard to equal. Passing through the war period with strikes and profiteers all around them, they did not lose their head, but listened to the advice of their superiors, who, on several occasions, took the time to get them altogether and talk to them. Then again, during the readjustment period they have demonstrated the confidence they have in their Boss. Not a whimper has been heard from the working men and women of our factory because they knew there was a very good reason for adjusting their wages, otherwise it would not have been done.

No Class Distinction at Lloyd's.

Mr. Lloyd is on speaking terms with all his workmen. No workman in our factory hesitates to speak to him and it is a pleasure to him to have a chat with some of the old cronies. The reason is they have seen him at work at all hours of the day and night when it became necessary for the welfare of his company. They look upon him as a pal and not a tyrant who would glory in their misfortune.

Lloyd's Hobby Is Concentration.

In all lectures to the employes Mr. Lloyd has recommended brain development and given instructive advice how to accomplish things worth while. In some cases it has already shown results as there are several young men who already have gained notoriety through lessons learned while working under the Big Chief.

Lloyd Is Handicapped.

We, the employes, have listened at different times to Mr. Lloyd's story and want to express the impressions they have left upon us.

First, we compare the voice to the physical structure which contains it. A wonderful contrast, isn't it? We feel that it must have required great effort to produce such a wonderful voice from so small a body.

Second, as we follow him in his discourse we hear things we do not hear elsewhere. They are different and as we follow him in his lecture he tells us why "he has learned to concentrate his thoughts. "When he sets about to think about a subject there is no power on earth that can detract his attention. This is the result of many years of hard sincere effort.

Is Self Made Man.

Mr. Lloyd capitalized his first success, namely—a loud voice, by selling different kinds of merchandise. However, he soon discovered that a loud voice must be substantiated by broad shoulders or a big brain. He began earnest concentration of thought. He labored day and night until he became master of his brain. Today he is now

THE SPEED KING

He weaves wickers thirty times faster than his competitors

as one of the world's greatest inventors and thinkers. His efforts have earned him millions of dollars, not by receiving more than others for his wares, but by selling his goods that are the best in the world for less money than they can be bought elsewhere. He did not take it out of our pockets as we know we have received the highest wages in the Twin Cities.

Capitalizes Inventions.

By careful business methods he has capitalized his inventions which developed from concentration of thought to such an extent that today all nations are helping all his coffers.

In religion he is very liberal and is welcome in all our churches, both Protestant and Catholic. Many of our ministers and priests are proud of calling our Chief their Pal. His benevolent work is done in secret as he abhors publicity on the subject. To give our readers a better idea of the inner man we will quote the answer of the Big Chief to a question asked him some time ago, namely:

"What do you consider the greatest thing you have accomplished?"

He said, "When I walk through the factory and see how many happy men and women are at work and the conditions they work under I feel the satisfaction of knowing that I have done some good for my fellow men."

In closing we want to tell a little story which Mr. Lloyd enjoys telling. His father operated a water power sawmill. Some trivial repairs were necessary and Marshall was selected to do the job. In doing so he accidentally fell dangerously near the wheel. After being rescued by his father, listen what he was told: "In the future you stay away from this mill. You are only good for holding things anyway."

Now dear readers, if it is possible for a man so handicapped—a small body, as poor as a church mouse, without education and pronounced by the father as only good for holding things—to make such a wonderful success by concentrating his thoughts, let us get started as we have the benefit of his experience.

GARDNER MEN ON VISIT

Mr. Brown and Mr. Goodspeed of the Gardner plant, the former a chemist and superintendent of the School Furniture Department, the latter efficiency expert and superintendent of the Mechanical department, paid us a two days' visit studying our production methods in the Stake department. They paid you a compliment, fellow working men and women, by stating that of all the different factories they had visited they had never seen such an intelligent lot of people.

George Rowell is spending his vacation at various northern Michigan lakes.

HURRAH, WE'RE ALL READY FOR THE BIG PICNIC

3 Big Boxing Bouts Windup
Jack Dempsey vs. Black
Jack Johnson.

Everyone pack your lunches and be ready to board the Lloyd special cars bound for Henes Park and enjoy yourself at the bigger and better than ever Lloyd picnic to be held on Saturday, Aug. 13. Music, dancing, racing and boxing galore

Marinette Lloyd special car will leave lower Hall avenue at 9 A. M., pass down Main street, across Menekaune bridge to Henes Park.

Menominee Lloyd special car will leave West Menominee from Stephenson avenue and Bellevue at 9:15 A. M., up Ogden avenue to Main street and north to Henes Park.

Menominee's city band will furnish music throughout the day and evening.

Lemonade and ice cream cones will be furnished free of charge as well as street car transportation.

Do not forget that every employe is urged to bring his or her entire family along, the more the merrier.

The day's events will be as follows:

11 A. M. sharp at baseball grounds.

Baseball.

North Shop vs. South Shop. Foremen vs. Office.

Winners of above games will play for factory championship.

Immediately following baseball games eat your lunches and hurry back to the baseball grounds so that we can begin the contest promptly at 2 P. M.

The athletic events are as follows, each winner to receive a prize:

Running race for boys under 16 years of age.

Running race for boys under 11 years of age.

Running race for girls under 16 years of age.

Running race for girls under 11 years of age.

Sack race for boys under 16 years of age.

Sack race for boys under 11 years of age.

Running race for married ladies.

Free for all running race for ladies and girls

Free for all running race for men and boys.

Egg and spoon race for girls under 16 years of age

Egg and spoon race for girls over 16 years of age.

Three legged race for boys under 16 years.

Three legged race for boys under 11 years.

Wheelbarrow race free for all.

Shoe race for ladies.

Shoe race for men.

Immediately following the races we are going to have a high class boxing exhibition, consisting of three matches between some of the best talent in Menominee. The bouts will also take

(Continued on Page Four)

In the years following the patenting of his loom, Marshall Lloyd branched out into the competitive field of wicker furniture. Recognizing that the public had preferred the closely woven style of wicker since 1910, he began to mass-produce machine-made wicker furniture of this type. At first, many of the established manufacturers of wicker furniture tried to compete with the Lloyd Manufacturing Company by producing closely woven furniture themselves, but they soon found that, because of the cost of labor and the great amount of time involved in producing this type of wicker by hand, it was not a very profitable business—not in competition with the Lloyd loom, which was capable

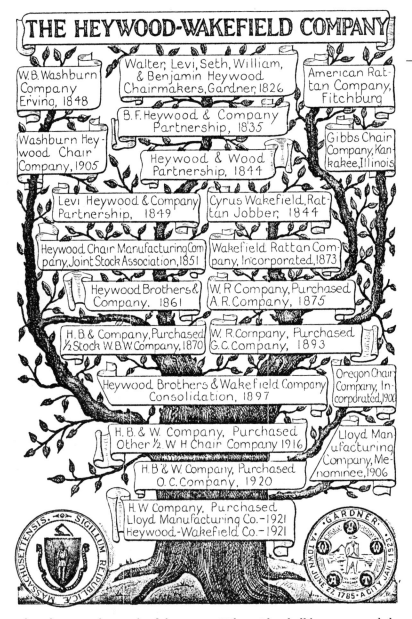

THE HEYWOOD-WAKEFIELD COMPANY

W.B. Washburn Company, Erving, 1848

Walter, Levi, Seth, William, & Benjamin Heywood, Chairmakers, Gardner, 1826

American Rattan Company, Fitchburg

B.F. Heywood & Company Partnership, 1835

Washburn Heywood Chair Company, 1905

Gibbs Chair Company, Kankakee, Illinois

Heywood & Wood Partnership, 1844

Levi Heywood & Company Partnership, 1849

Cyrus Wakefield, Rattan Jobber, 1844

Heywood Chair Manufacturing Company, Joint Stock Association, 1851

Wakefield Rattan Company, Incorporated, 1873

Heywood Brothers & Company, 1861

W.R Company, Purchased A.R. Company, 1875

H.B. & Company, Purchased ½ Stock W.B.W. Company, 1870

W.R. Company, Purchased G.C. Company, 1893

Heywood Brothers & Wakefield Company Consolidation, 1897

Oregon Chair Company, Incorporated, 1900

H.B. & W. Company, Purchased Other ½ W H Chair Company 1916

Lloyd Manufacturing Company, Menominee, 1906

H.B. & W. Company, Purchased O.C. Company, 1920

H.W. Company, Purchased Lloyd Manufacturing Co. – 1921 – Heywood-Wakefield Co. – 1921

The roots of the Heywood-Wakefield Company are traced in this family tree.

of performing the work of thirty men! Thus, Lloyd all but cornered the market on the popular closely woven wicker from 1917 until 1921, when his company was bought out and became a wholly owned subsidiary of Heywood-Wakefield Company (the simplification of the company's corporate title coincided with the purchase of Lloyd Manufacturing Company). At this point the evolution of the Heywood-Wakefield Company was converted into a visual "family tree" by a company artist, and it became exceedingly evident that the firm had quite an interesting heritage.

At this time, the three main factories divided responsibilities. The

Gardner factory housed the lumberyard, designing department, wood-shop, carriage department, and chemical laboratory. The Wakefield factory housed the cane-weaving machinery, car-seating department, and matting department. And the seventeen-acre Menominee factory housed the fiber-spinning department (including a figure-eight braiding machine and a shaped fabric loom), metalworking department, weaving room, and upholstery department.

In purchasing Lloyd's company, Heywood-Wakefield Company showed that they were fully aware of the challenges of the industry and had accepted the forms and materials of mass production. It was a wise move on the part of Heywood-Wakefield, for they now owned the Lloyd loom patent and they knew that in the years ahead there would be far greater use of fiber as the material for machine-woven furniture. Indeed, in 1912 only 15 percent of all wicker furniture was made of fiber, but by 1920 this figure had risen to almost 50 percent; by the late 1920s fiber was used in the production of 80 percent of all wicker furniture made in America.

With twelve Lloyd loom machines going at once, the Heywood-Wakefield Company reemphasized its prominence in the wicker industry. In 1922 the British firm of W. Lusty & Sons purchased a license from the Heywood-Wakefield Company to make Lloyd loom wicker furniture in Britain. Although this firm developed some of their own designs, their classic twenties pieces were drawn directly from Heywood-Wakefield trade catalogs.

During the 1920s the wicker furniture industry made use of Art Deco design principles. Named for an exhibition held in Paris in 1925, "L'Exposition International des Arts Décoratifs," the Art Deco designs in wicker furniture were based on rational construction, simple ornamentation, and geometric lines. Striving for harmony and balance of design, wicker manufacturers began producing pieces with conservative curving lines that were dictated by proportion and good taste. The

Lloyd loom wicker furnished the tearoom of the luxury liner **Viceroy of India** *in the early 1920s.*

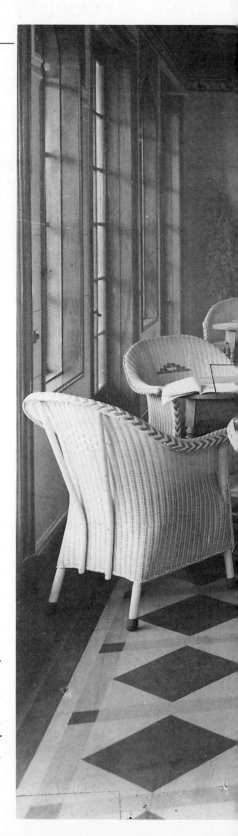

new Art Deco wicker was functional and possessed a general harmony of design, yet many of the chairs and settees relied on removable innerspring seats for comfort, rather than on wickerwork. The famous diamond design woven into the backs of most Art Deco wicker has become one of the key points to look for when identifying wicker furniture from the 1920s. On many of the better-quality examples these diamond patterns were painted or stained a contrasting color at the factory to produce a strong visual effect and a three-dimensional quality.

The twenties saw a greater amount of wicker floor and table lamps, porch swings, library tables, tea carts, buffets, and china cabinets. Designers continued to perfect wicker phonograph cabinets and also introduced the "Lomodi," the predecessor of today's hide-a-bed. Promotional pieces also gained their share of attention, one of the most notable being the "Lloyd Flyer" baby carriage, which was a surefire favorite during the Lindbergh era, for obvious reasons.

Although wicker imports were still available in the twenties, there were considerably fewer on the market; once again, the vast quantity of fine wicker furniture was being made in America. However, the legacy of heavily upholstered European wicker lived on in American wicker design, and many pieces relied on innerspring seats and cushioned backs that were usually covered with brightly colored prints. The twenties also saw the widespread use and acceptance of such money-saving practices as using turned wood framework that at first glance looked like wrapped cane. Gesso roses and flower wreaths became popular during this decade. More than ever before wicker manufacturers increased their use of inexpensive materials such as Oriental sea grass and prairie grass. Both materials were hand-twisted and displayed variegated green and tan colors. Unlike fiber, Oriental sea grass and prairie grass were not adaptable to a mechanical loom and dictated handweaving.

Late in that decade wicker furniture quickly began to lose its long-held popularity with the public. Disenchanted wicker buyers turned their backs on machine-made, mass-produced pieces, longing for the

The popular diamond design was sometimes painted a darker color to make it stand out, as on some of these 1920 pieces from the Heywood-Wakefield salesroom in Chicago.

The "Lloyd Flyer" baby carriage was the brainchild of the advertising department at the Heywood-Wakefield Company and was intended for exhibition only. It was made of fiber and had a small motor hidden inside the body of the plane that was attached to a battery which turned the propeller at a slow speed.

LLOYD SHOP NEWS

PUBLISHED BY AND FOR THE WORKERS AT THE LLOYD FACTORY

VOLUME 8   MENOMINEE, MICHIGAN, SEPTEMBER 25, 1926   NUMBER 4

HARVEST DANCE WILL USHER IN FALL PROGRAM

October 22 Is Date Chosen for Big Ball; All Must Dress Like Rubes.

Lloyd workers are in line for one of the best entertainments ever given for them, when, on Friday evening, October 22, the fall and winter dance season will be ushered in at the Menominee Legion hall with a gala harvest ball. It is going to be a real "hard-times" party with everyone dressed as "hay-seeds," or in other "hick" attire. A decorating committee will transform the Legion hall into a harvest setting. A special orchestra from "Bloomerville" has been engaged and nothing is being left undone to make it one of the finest evenings in the history of Lloyd entertainments.

Great Crowd Expected

Everybody's going to this party and everyone must come dressed as "hay-seeds." Those coming in city clothes will be asked to look on from the hay loft. The older folks, as well as the younger people, will be there in large number to share in the fun.

The athletic committee, under whose supervision recreation and athletics are being held, are attempting one of the biggest things ever given before in the line of entertainments and they want every worker to help make it a success. An advance ticket sale will be instituted to insure its success.

To Be Gala Event

The committee in charge of the event requested the following letter printed in the Shop News that all may know what a fine time is in store for them:

Lloyd Flyer Makes Big Hit

Here is another piece of evidence that this company is leading the field, both in new ideas and better baby carriages. This is not one of the latest numbers in carriage styles, but just a novel creation constructed to make dealers "sit up and take notice" of what is being done to encourage greater enthusiasm in baby carriage sales.

Only the "wide-awake" manufacturer is able to hold its own in the industrial field today. That, along with the fact that the American public likes to be startled by seeing something different and sensational are reasons why this aeroplane was built for exhibition purposes by designers in the factory.

It was on exhibition at the Lloyd space during the summer market in July at Chicago. Hundreds of dealers and others, who visited the Lloyd display, marveled at the sight of this unique baby carriage flyer. It created a great impression with everyone who saw it.

The aeroplane was built by adding a tail, wings, propeller and guy wires to a stock pullman carriage. It is built entirely of fiber with the exception of the chassis and the hangar supporting the propeller. A small motor hidden in the body of the plane, which can either be attached to a battery or an electric light socket, revolves the propeller at a slow speed. The entire plane is finished in an attractive copper color which sets it off nicely.

The idea, originating from the Advertising department, was partly prompted by the success experienced with the auto carriage, which was received with enthusiasm in many sections of the country. The plane was exhibited recently in San Francisco, where it made a decided hit with the public on the coast. Several of the leading newspapers in that city ran a picture with an interesting news story in one of their issues.

The aeroplane was received by the dealers more enthusiastically than the auto carriage, since it was considerably more novel and sensational. Many of the dealers were disappointed in learning that the flyer was purely for exhibitional use, but nevertheless they were glad to see this company retaining the lead in new advertising methods and finer carriages.

FRANK PSCHEID IS NEW WESTERN INSPECTOR HERE

Assumed His New Duties On Aug. 1; Was Chief Clerk at Local R. R. Office.

Frank Pscheid, a local young man and former star on the Menominee High school football team back in 1916, is the new factory representative of the Western Weighing & Inspection Bureau. He was appointed to succeed Irving Kaul, who worked here several months after Charles H. Brandecker was transferred to Milwaukee. Frank took over his new duties August 1, having been previously employed by The Chicago, Milwaukee & St. Paul Railroad as chief clerk at their local freight office.

To many of the workers throughout the plant Frank needs no introduction, as he is not altogether a stranger here. Many will remember him when he worked in the Wood department after his graduation from Menominee High. Others, more especially those who have followed the high school's gridiron records, will remember him when he played football.

On Winning Team

By hard practice he won the position of right tackle on the high school eleven. He was a regular on the team in '16 and '17. In 1916, his first year on the squad, Menominee was successful in defeating their rivals, Marinette, by a 3 to 6 score. His work on

LUSTY HERE FROM LONDON, SACK JOE SMALTER'S FORD

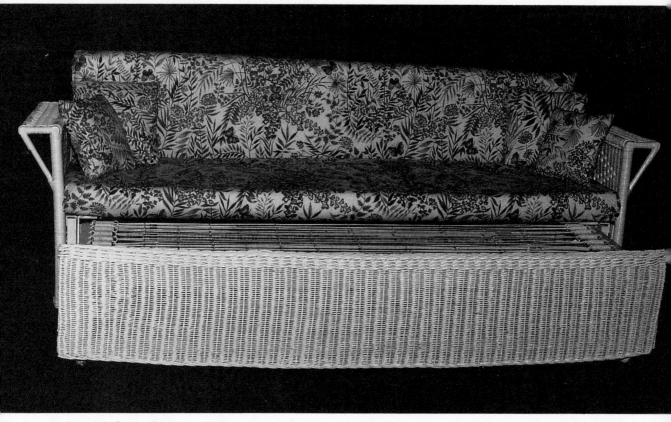

A Lomodi from the late 1920s.

The company's newsletter refused to accept the reality of the situation even in the midst of the Depression (right).

uniquely individual feel wicker had once possessed. The manufacturers felt the decline in sales and realized that the entire industry was in deep trouble. They stepped up their advertising campaigns, using elaborate artwork, and tried new styles such as "stick wicker" (a short-lived style that emphasized harsh vertical lines with thick round reed), but nothing seemed to work. Sales continued to drop at an alarming rate. Industry insiders refused to accept the reality of the situation, but the hard facts were staring them in the face. The end was clearly in sight.

Two major factors led to the downfall of the wicker furniture industry in the early 1930s, and they went hand in hand: the Lloyd loom and Art Deco. With the advent of machine-made closely woven wicker there was an initial surge of popularity, but after a few years the public slowly began to feel that true craftsmanship had vanished from the wicker furniture industry. Perhaps the strongest tie between this

The Lloyd Loominator

PUBLISHED MONTHLY FOR LLOYD DEALERS

July, 1932   MENOMINEE, MICHIGAN   No. 111

LLOYD LANDS SOLAR PLEXUS BLOW; DEPRESSION GRUNTS!

THE SIX ROUND BUSINESS BOUT
JAN · FEB · MARCH · APRIL · MAY · JUNE
LLOYD WINS BY K.O.

LLOYD

OLD MAN DEPRESSION

In the
FIRST SIX MONTHS

From the very start of 1932's "Battle for Business", Old Man Depression sensed he had a lively foe.

That first round—The January Market—had experts arguing pro and con. Some said Lloyd couldn't keep up the pace of a 52.2% gain in volume. Others said Lloyd was just getting "warmed up". Buyers kept out of the argument; they were too busy selecting from the Lloyd Carriage line, the Lloydspring Outdoor line and the Lloyd Fibre Furniture line.

Now that the first six "rounds" are "all over but the shouting", the boys in the press box will tell you they knew it all along. "Why, the Depression couldn't lick Lloyd," they say, "Those best buys in carriages were miles ahead of competition. And that Lloydspring Outdoor Furniture!—it had them all stopped. When Lloyd really sets out to win business, it wins it!"

For the
NEXT SIX MONTHS

Lloyd's been preparing a long time to put over another real victory in the second six-month's Battle for Business. There's been a lot of secret planning going on. Lloyd Merchandisers, Designers a n d Factory Superintendents have talked and planned into the early hours of many mornings to get the campaign worked out just right. Pencils have been sharpened as never before in figuring costs. There are plenty of new things up our sleeves that we can't show until market time. But you can just mark this down in your little book:

The dealers who put confidence in Lloyd lines this Summer and Fall are going to be "in the money" when this year's Business Battle is over. There'll be New Ideas, New Values, N e w Merchandising Helps, New Merchandise, New Profit Possibilities. The gong sounds soon for the first round at the Summer Market. Next December you, too, will say, "I told you so."

furniture and the American public had always been the fact that it was handmade. Moreover, the Art Deco style, which readily accepted machine and mass production, only added to public discontent. Had manufacturers been more attuned to the art of handmade wicker furniture and not merely to sales figures, they might have realized that the industry had lost touch with its roots. Originally the most popular aspect of wicker furniture had been its elasticity and ability to give with the weight of its user. If construction had been kept on a high level of craftsmanship, the magic of wicker might have continued hypnotizing future generations. However, it was not meant to be. The early thirties

Wicker rockers, armchairs, and settees from the 1927 Heywood-Wakefield catalog.

82
Upholstered
Wicker
Fireside
Chairs

Heywood-Wakefield
TRADE MARK

W 163 CU-1
Reed Seat
Width—20 inches   Depth—22 inches
Height of Back—34 inches

W 163 DU-1
Reed Seat
Width—20 inches   Depth—22 inches
Height of Back—34 inches

W 71 CU
Sleepy Hollow Chair
Reed Seat
Width—20 inches   Depth—20 inches
Height of Back—31 inches

W 163 CU-2
Reed Seat
Width—20 inches   Depth—22 inches
Height of Back—34 inches

W 163 DU-2
Reed Seat
Width—20 inches   Depth—22 inches
Height of Back—34 inches
FOR FINISHES SEE PAGE 5

W 174 CU
Sleepy Hollow Chair
Reed Seat
Width—21 inches   Depth—24 inches
Height of Back—36 inches

witnessed the death of a once thriving industry, as well as a totally unique, functional art form.

The true "art" of wicker furniture was lost in the transition from highly skilled craftsmen, using their hands to produce unbelievably ornate designs with two, three, and sometimes four different types of natural material, to the use of a machine that could weave only the most basic of designs and was limited to the use of man-made fiber.

Probably the last wicker designs to gain wide public acceptance before the downfall of the industry are those shown in the 1927 Heywood-Wakefield Company trade catalogs.

Heywood-Wakefield

81
Upholstered
Wicker
Fireside
Chairs

W 161 CU-1
Reed Seat
Width—20½ inches   Depth—21 inches
Height of Back—29 inches

W 161 FU-1
Reed Seat
Width—42 inches   Depth—21½ inches
Height of Back—28½ inches

W 161 DU-1
Reed Seat
Width—20½ inches   Depth—21 inches
Height of Back—27 inches

W 161 CU-2
Reed Seat
Width—21½ inches   Depth—21 inches
Height of Back—29 inches

W 161 DU-2
Reed Seat
Width—20½ inches   Depth—21 inches
Height of Back—27 inches

FOR FINISHES SEE PAGE 5

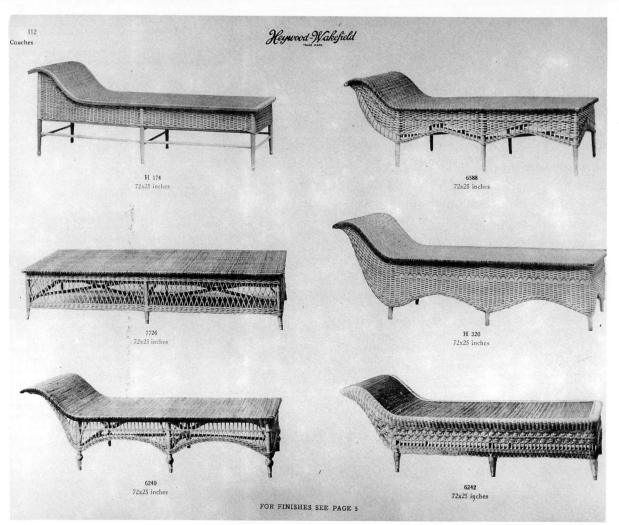

Wicker couches from the 1927 Heywood-Wakefield catalog.

Wicker tea carts from the 1927 Heywood-Wakefield catalog.

*Wicker lamps from the 1927
Heywood-Wakefield catalog.*

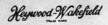

Heywood-Wakefield
TRADE MARK

W 8199
Electric Lamp
Chain Pull Socket for One Light. 20 inches
High, Shade 14 inches Diameter. Wired and
Fitted with 6-foot Silk Covered Cord and Elec-
tric Plug. Lined with French Cretonne or
China Silk.

Electric Lamp with Cane Panels
Chain Pull Socket for One Light. 19 inches
High, Shade 12½x12½ inches. Wired and Fit-
ted with 6-foot Silk Covered Cord and Electric
Plug. Lined with French Cretonne or China
Silk.

W 8265
Electric Lamp
Chain Pull Socket for One Light. 22 inches
High, Shade 14½ inches Diameter. Wired and
Fitted with 6-foot Silk Covered Cord and Elec-
tric Plug. Lined with French Cretonne or
China Silk.

W 8264
Electric Lamp
Chain Pull Socket for One Light. 26 inches
High, Shade 18 inches Diameter. Wired and
Fitted with 6-foot Silk Covered Cord and Elec-
tric Plug. Lined with French Cretonne or
China Silk.

W 8266
Electric Lamp
Chain Pull Socket for One Light. 25 inches
High, Shade 14x14 inches. Wired and Fitted
with 6-foot Silk Covered Cord and Electric
Plug. Lined with French Cretonne or China
Silk.

W 8204
Oil Lamp
25 inches High, Shade 16 inches Diameter.
Fitted with Rochester Burner. Lined with
French Cretonne or China Silk.

W 8268
Electric Lamp
Chain Pull Sockets for Two Lights. 27½
inches High, Shade 19 inches Diameter. Wired
and Fitted with 6-foot Silk Covered Cord and
Electric Plug. Lined with French Cretonne
or China Silk.

FOR FINISHES SEE PAGE 5

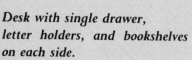

A PORTFOLIO OF WICKER FURNITURE

THE TWENTIES

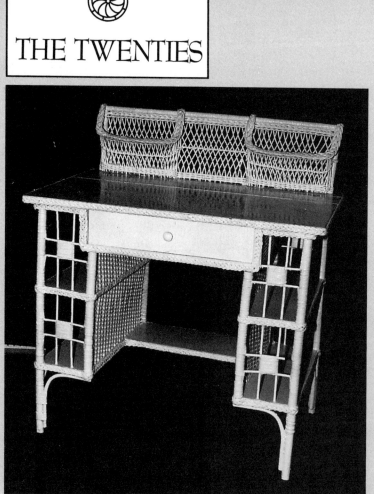

Desk with single drawer, letter holders, and bookshelves on each side.

*Table lamp
from the late 1920s.*

Armchair from the early 1920s.

Wicker tea cart.

Wicker side chair (above). Wood and reed armchair (right) from the turn of the century.

Two examples of wicker rockers from the twenties. The popular Bar Harbor wicker rocker made of reed (above). Upholstered rocker made of fiber (right).

Four examples of wicker armchairs from the twenties. Tightly woven reed armchair (above). Bar Harbor armchair with pineapple feet (above right). Upholstered armchair handmade of fiber (below). A wingback chair with magazine rack side pockets (right).

Three styles of wicker chaise longues. Upholstered chaise longue with magazine rack side pockets (above). Upholstered, tightly woven longue with open back (right). Classic Bar Harbor–style chaise longue (below).

Two wicker desks from the twenties.

*Round wicker table and
four matching straight-back chairs.*

Various styles of wicker lamps.

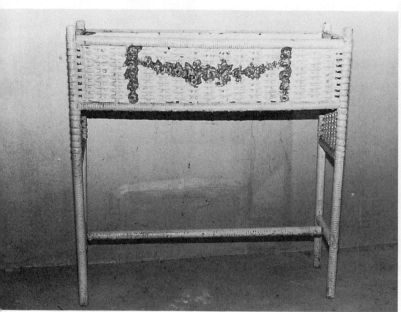

Plant stand with gesso wreath and flower work over closely woven body.

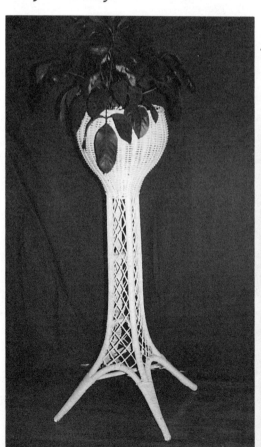

Tall fernery.

Wicker hat rack or clothes tree.

Common rectangular plant stand with metal liner.

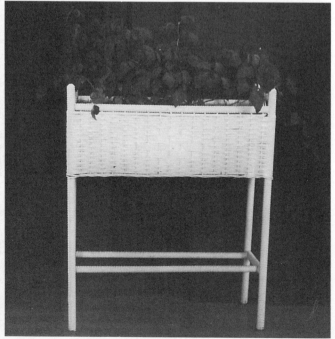

Wicker picture frames.

Tightly woven wicker bed frame.

Small bedside table.

*Children's wicker from
the twenties. Child's
rocker made of fiber
(left). Buggy (above)
with adjustable hood.*

*Rocker handmade of
fiber with cushioned seat
(right).*

Turkish bench with innerspring cushion.

Matching rocker and armchair with ottoman from the early 1920s.

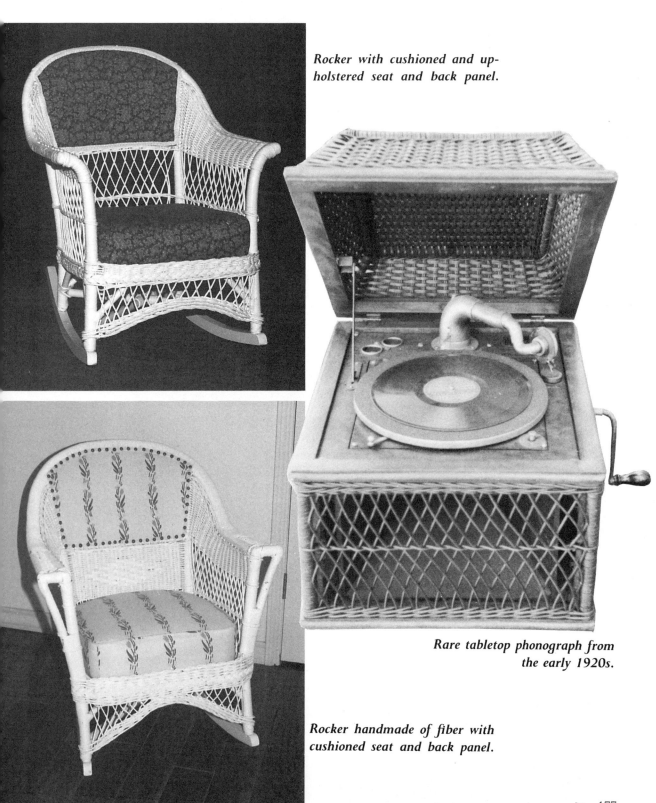

Rocker with cushioned and upholstered seat and back panel.

Rare tabletop phonograph from the early 1920s.

Rocker handmade of fiber with cushioned seat and back panel.

Desk and chair handmade of fiber.

Oblong table and two side chairs made of fiber.

Floor lamp with figure-eight braiding.

Twin beds (above) made of reed with diamond designs and curved footboards. Double bed (below) with openwork window design and closely woven diamond pattern.

Oak gateleg table (above). Magazine rack (right) with diamond design in center and full-length handle.

Library table with storage shelves at each end (below). Five feet in length with oak top.

The Twenties ➤ 181

Elaborate plant stand with four metal-lined planters and hanging birdcage.

Desk set from the late 1920s.

Plant stand with metal liner.

Bridge lamp with fringe-lined shade and two small shelves.

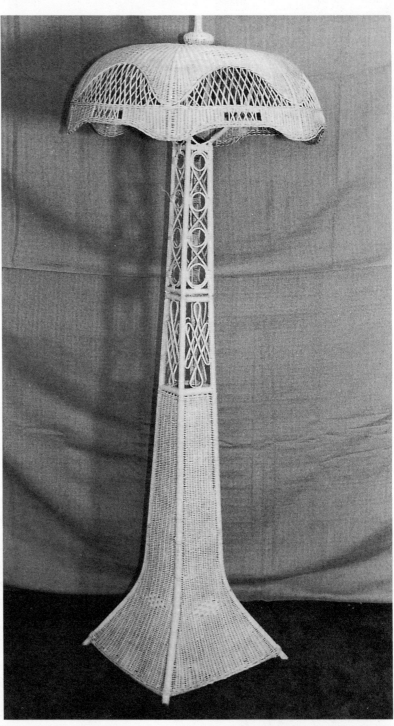

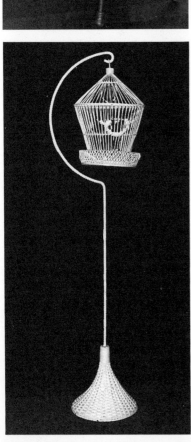

Birdcage and stand from the early 1920s.

Floor lamp with attractive shade and closely woven base.

Table lamp with applied lattice-work on base.

Stylish table lamp with original fringe under shade.

Two-bulb table lamp from the early 1920s.

Buffets, with three silverware drawers and two storage compartments (above). With two drawers and two large side storage compartments (right). Another example from the late 1920s (below).

Portable sewing cabinet with double-door entry.

Uniquely designed settee with scalloped reed fancywork and cushioned seat.

Quilt rack (left) with closely woven top.

Round table (far left) with circular woven top and bottom shelf.

Chest of drawers (right) with diamond design and oak top.

Gateleg dining table and four matching chairs wrapped with fiber.

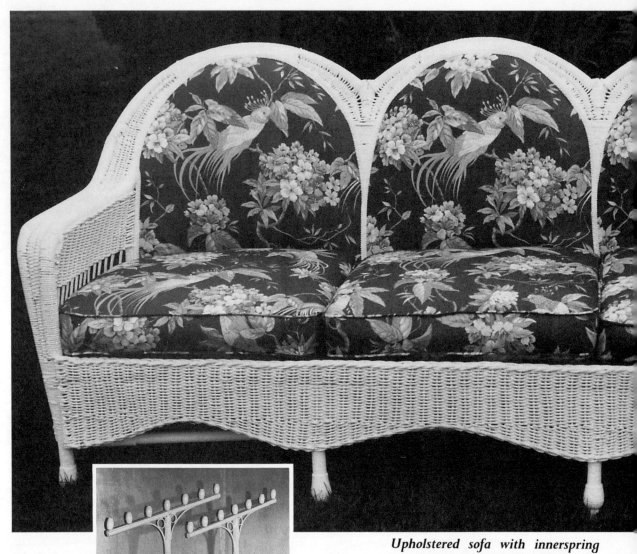

Upholstered sofa with innerspring seating and padded backrests.

Two candle holders.

Art Deco—style sewing basket.

Bar Harbor—style buffet with three drawers.

Electrified candlestick holders (left) made of plied reed.

Rare buffet server (far left) with four glass-paneled cupboards, three silverware drawers, and two storage compartments.

Smoking stand (left) with arched handle and metal ashtray, which includes matchbox holder.

Rare secretary (above) with diamond designs stained green, cylindrical rolltop opens to desk, bookcase above with two glass doors.

Classic 1920 baby carriage with closely woven adjustable hood.

Punch server with center metal canister for punch and outer wicker area designed for glasses.

Punch server with lift-off glass tray and bottom shelf.

Vanity with three-way mirror and three drawers.

China cabinet with center glass door and two glass side panels.

Tea cart with lift-off woven tray and three bottom shelves.

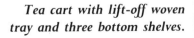

6
Buying Antique Wicker Furniture

urchasing wicker furniture for your home can give an otherwise boring and predictable interior the romanticism, style, and comfort of a bygone era. Quality wicker from the Victorian era, the turn of the century, and the twenties possesses a nostalgic charm and verve that are undeniable. Interior decorators have used fine old wicker for decades as informal accent pieces, but within the past ten years it has made a quantum jump—now complete sets of wicker have invaded the living rooms, dining rooms, and bedrooms of some of the most trend-setting homes in America.

Where to Find Wicker

inding antique wicker is getting harder all the time. Geographically the eastern and midwestern states have more wicker to choose from, since most of the large companies were located there, but it is available practically everywhere. The days of finding old wicker stored in attics or barns is all but over. If Aunt Mary didn't know that her wicker was worth something ten years ago, you can almost bet that friends have set her straight by now, or offered to buy it up

Victorian wicker picture frame.

Doll stroller (left) with acorn spools, adjustable back, and footrest, from the 1890s.

Victorian bedside table.

themselves. Of course, if you hustle and luck is on your side you can still come across a real bargain now and then, and that has always been the exciting part of collecting wicker.

Whether you are building an entire collection of antique wicker or simply decking out a cozy sun porch, one of the best sources for finding quality pieces is a wicker specialty shop (see Appendix 3). Not only do the shop owners carry a large selection of fine wicker furniture, but they are an invaluable source of information. As specialists in the field, these dealers usually answer difficult questions about wicker and provide information concerning the rarity, style, and value of a given piece. Their expertise enables them to obtain the finest wicker pieces available from across the country.

Antiques shops can also unearth good wicker bargains and should be frequented regularly. Antiques shows and flea markets can provide some very good pieces, but be advised that the best way of protecting yourself from overpriced wicker or reproductions is to know your wicker furniture. Once armed with a wide knowledge of your specialization, you can actually be one up on weekend dealers at flea markets and garage sales. Keep in mind that shows and fleas are a good place to meet people with similar interests and exchange sources and information.

Antiques auctions can also turn up some good deals in wicker, but the prospective buyer should thoroughly examine the merchandise at the auction preview. Inspect pieces under consideration with a cool, logical eye and search for any damage to the wickerwork, structural weakness, or poorly repaired areas. These previews give you the advantage of making a calm decision before you are carried away by the contagious excitement generated at most auctions.

WHAT TO LOOK FOR WHEN BUYING WICKER

Factors to consider before you buy a piece of wicker include comfort, the beauty of the design, strength of the framework, quality of materials, the age, rarity, and the overall craftsmanship. Natural, or unpainted, wicker is far more desirable than painted wicker and is highly prized by serious collectors. If you choose to buy a painted piece, avoid overpainted examples.

Sometimes an excellent piece of wicker in need of repair will come on the market, and the prospective buyer should not be scared off if the damage is restricted to the wickerwork and the frame is still in good condition. Some basic repair methods for the layman are outlined in Chapter 7. For difficult jobs, contact a professional wicker restoration specialist (see Appendix 2). These artisans can work miracles and greatly enhance the value of a piece.

A Word about Reproductions

The ability to detect wicker reproductions is an important skill to develop for the collector of antique wicker furniture. One of the main problems I have run across in restoring wicker furniture for the public is the general confusion in identifying old wicker and spotting reproductions. Some reproductions from the Far East can be a problem for the beginner because the designs are usually Victorian in nature, with flowing lines and curlicues. There are,

Victorian rocker with tennis racket motif set into backrest.

Turkish bench from the 1890s.

Ornate Victorian armchair employing five-legged design and figure-eight fancywork covering arms and back.

however, a few key points to look for if you are not sure whether a piece is old or a reproduction. The seats on reproduction wicker chairs are never cane seats with wooden frames, but rather flimsy, circular-woven reed seats. These seats are usually a dead giveaway, and more often than not they are damaged and falling through the framework because of their poor construction and design. Reproductions are also much lighter than old wicker pieces, because the framework is made of bamboo or rattan rather than solid hardwoods. Another clue is the poor quality of the reeds used in imported reproductions; they are fibrous and usually very brittle and dry-looking. Visit some import shops that carry new wicker furniture. You'll see that it doesn't take an expert to tell the difference between a fraud and the real thing. Once you develop a feel for spotting antique wicker furniture your confidence in buying it will grow.

DATING WICKER FURNITURE

Because age is one of the prime considerations when buying wicker, most collectors concentrate on pre-1930 pieces. While it is virtually impossible to pinpoint the exact date of manufacture, it is possible to come up with an educated guess based on style. The three distinct eras of wicker furniture (Victorian, turn-of-the-century, and the twenties) were known for their distinct styles and design techniques. Although dating a piece by style alone is never completely accurate, it should be used as one of many important bits of evidence. Old wicker trade catalogs can also be valuable in dating pieces, but it should be remembered that some popular designs were made over a twenty-year period, simply because they were good sellers. And company labels can offer important clues to the era of manufacture. Although the majority of labels were paper and have disappeared with age, some have withstood the ravages of time. Aside from paper labels, there were metal and celluloid labels attached under the framework of the seat, to the back of the seat, or on one of the cross braces under the seat. These can provide valuable leads in tracking down the era of a specific piece. The label will mention not only the company but also the factory location.

Regarding labels from the famous Heywood-Wakefield Company and its predecessors, any piece of wicker bearing a label with the

Heywood or Wakefield name should be given extra consideration. These companies still carry the reputation of an entire industry. Since they had distinctive dates of operation, the following guidelines should help place these pieces in the correct time frame:

Wakefield Rattan Company	1855–97
Heywood Brothers and Company	1868–97
Heywood Brothers & Wakefield Company	1897–1921
Heywood-Wakefield Company	1921–

(The company name was *officially* shortened to "Heywood-Wakefield" in 1921; however, it began showing up on a limited number of celluloid labels around the turn of the century, often in combination with the red-and-white "Heywood Brothers & Wakefield Company" paper labels.)

Four-tiered bookcase from the turn of the century.

WICKER AS AN INVESTMENT

Every investor in the antique wicker field should strive for pieces that combine overall quality (in design, materials, and workmanship), rarity, age, and good condition. All of these count heavily when entering the rarefied air of collecting for investment. The beauty of wicker furniture is that it is both a work of art and a functional object. Part of the pleasure of investing in an exceptional piece of wicker is that it can be used and admired daily.

Regardless of whether it exhibits a mahogany stain, the "fancy colored reeds" popular in Victorian times, or the "duo-tone" paint jobs so much in evidence during the 1920s, a wicker piece exhibiting the original finish is by far the most desirable when buying with an eye toward investment.

Buying matching sets (such as a settee, armchair, rocker, and chaise longue of the same design and finish) is probably the best bet for today's investor. Beyond this, unique designs, such as Victorian "theme" chairs or rockers with woven back panels of quarter-moons, stars, banjos, hearts, or sailboats, have also proved to be good investments over the years.

7
RESTORING AND CARING FOR WICKER FURNITURE

WHY RESTORE ANTIQUE WICKER?

The restoration of antique wicker furniture has long been considered a lost art. Many people seem to think that once wicker is damaged, they cannot do anything about it. Nothing could be further from the truth. All wicker furniture can be restored in one degree or another, and usually there is a good chance of complete restoration unless the framework has rotted over the years. However, why restore antique wicker when reproductions of fancy Victorian wicker furniture are available at lower prices?

The answer is that antique wicker is far more durable, in both structure and design, than the wicker reproductions being made today. The quality of the materials employed in both the framework and the weaving is far superior to that used in modern reproductions. There is also the fact that a truly old piece of wicker furniture is considered an antique, and any antique is worth restoring to its original state. The value of antique wicker in good condition is climbing at such an alarming rate that this furniture should be looked on as an investment, as well as beautiful and useful to own.

Side chair with cabriole legs from the 1900s and rocker from 1900 with rolled arms.

MATERIALS

Lady's Victorian armchair with two finely woven medallions in backrest.

The most common materials used in restoring wicker furniture: (1) round reed, (2) flat reed, (3) binding cane, (4) fiber, (5) sea grass.

Just as different types of materials were used in making wicker furniture, these materials also came in various sizes and shapes. Appendix 1 provides a list of the craft supply houses in the United States that carry wickerwork materials of all kinds. The best procedure is to write one of these companies and either ask for a price list of the wickerwork materials they have in stock or simply send a small sample of the material from a damaged piece and ask them to identify it and its size and tell you the price per pound or hank.

This illustration shows the most commonly used materials employed in the making of wicker furniture. The sources listed in Appendix 1 can supply all or at least some of these materials.

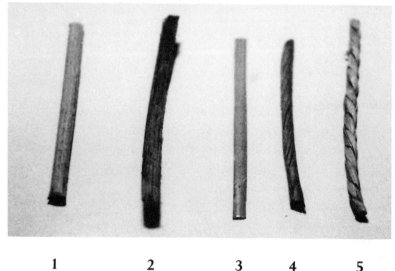

1 2 3 4 5

PREPARATION OF MATERIALS

Before attempting any wicker repair techniques, it is important to know that some materials must be prepared before they can be used.

REED

Either round or flat reed should be soaked in warm water before being used. Reed is a supple material when wet, but it will snap very easily if it is worked dry. A good rule to follow is this: the thicker the reed, the longer it should be soaked. Thinner reeds need only a three-minute soaking to become supple, whereas thick round reeds should be soaked for about ten minutes. It is important to soak only the amount of reed that will be used promptly, because reed frays and splits when left to soak for longer than thirty minutes.

CANE

Binding cane is used extensively in wrapping the framework of wicker furniture, but it should never be worked dry. Simply pass it through water quickly to make it supple and lessen the chances of its cracking. Cane that is shipped in a coil is sometimes difficult to straighten. If such proves to be the case, the entire coil should be soaked in warm water for a few minutes, then hung on a hook to drop out straight and dry. Cane should not be stored near heaters or hot pipes, as it will become brittle and break easily.

FIBER AND SEA GRASS

Both these materials should be worked dry. They are extremely supple in their natural state, and no preparation is necessary.

TOOLS

Here are the basic tools and related supplies needed to restore wicker furniture: a hammer; ½-inch to ¾-inch nails; glue (Weldwood or LePage's Original white glue is recommended); and a pair of sharp hand clippers or heavy scissors. An electric drill is also needed for some of the more difficult repair jobs. All tools and materials should be close at hand and arranged for convenient use.

Music stand from the Heywood Brothers & Wakefield Company.

TECHNIQUES OF WICKER RESTORATION

T he following pages illustrate some of the more basic wicker restoration techniques that can be mastered by the layman in a short time. The key word in trying your hand at some or all of these techniques is "patience." If you are patient and careful with your materials, there is no reason why you cannot restore your own wicker furniture.

WRAPPING

This chair leg needs to be rewrapped with binding cane. It is far easier to turn a chair over and work on it with the leg sticking up. After removing all nails from the bare wood, nail the loose cane to the wood, making sure that the nail is facing the inside of the chair so it will not be visible from the front.

The new length of cane is placed over the broken cane and nailed to the leg in the same manner.

The binding cane is wrapped tightly around the bare leg to within a half inch of the top. Then the same nailing procedure is used to fasten the end of it. Remember to always nail the cane on the inside so that the nail will not show when the chair is turned upright.

Both the top and bottom ends of the cane wrapping are cut close to the nail, and glue is spread over the freshly cut ends, next to the nails.

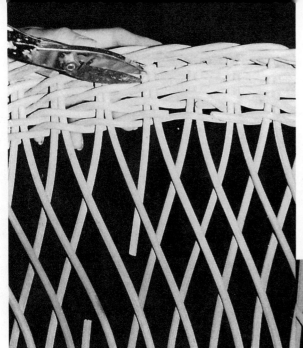

REPLACING SPOKES

To replace a broken vertical reed, or spoke, first remove the broken reed by snipping it off at the top, above the third or fourth row of the wooden horizontal reeds.

The bottom of the broken spoke must then be snipped out below the fourth row of the lower woven horizontal reeds.

A new spoke is fitted into place after it has been soaked. Note that all the spokes follow a pattern: those in the front slant one way and those in the back slant in the opposite direction. It is important to determine what the original pattern was and follow it as carefully as possible.

The new round reed spoke is inserted between the bottom rows of horizontal weaving. Then it is carefully bent in the middle so that the other end can be inserted between the weaving at the top of the chair. If the spoke does not slide through the horizontal weaving easily, don't force it; take the clippers and cut a sharp point on the tip of the spoke. This point should make it possible to push the spoke through the weaving with less resistance.

The end result should look like this. Gluing is not necessary in most cases.

LOCKING

One of the most common flaws in wicker furniture is a missing or damaged horizontal reed.

In order to replace a single horizontal reed, first snap the damaged reed off just under the spokes to the left and right. In this photo a screwdriver is inserted under the damaged reed and lifted up to snap off the reed directly under the spoke to the left. When it is possible to clip the horizontal reed from the back, I recommend doing so, but in this case (since the repair is on a hollow, serpentine back) a screwdriver and leverage had to be employed to snap the reed off.

Locking is the laying together of the ends of a weaving strand. The two ends of the new reed are inserted (left and right) under the cut-off ends of the old reed, thus forming a fastening.

The finished job. The new horizontal reed usually dries tightly in place, but glue is sometimes necessary to ensure a permanent bond.

This chair is fairly simple to repair because all the spokes are intact.

Don't be afraid to cut away loose or uneven reeds.

The under-and-over weave is simple. The first row to be rewoven should be the exact opposite of the last intact row above it. Here the new weave is started under the spoke because the reed directly above it begins by going over the first spoke.

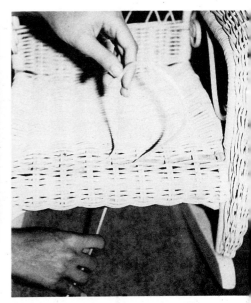

The under-and-over weave is well named, for the technique used in this weave consists of weaving over one spoke and under the next. One hand should be used as a guide to feed the reed to the other hand (under the seat), which pulls the reed slowly through.

The end result should look like this. A light coat of white glue spread over the repaired material is recommended to both strengthen the weave and seal the reed for painting.

COMBINING TECHNIQUES

Before attempting to restore a piece like this, be sure that you have mastered all the techniques illustrated up to this point. All the restoration techniques covered will be put to use on this job.

The first step is to clip out the damaged spokes.

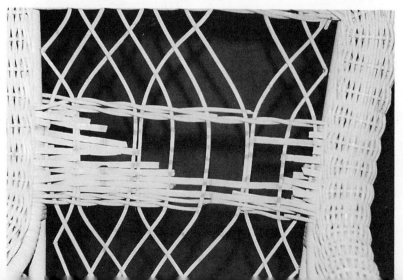

After damaged spokes are removed, study the design of the spokes to make sure that the restoration job duplicates the original pattern.

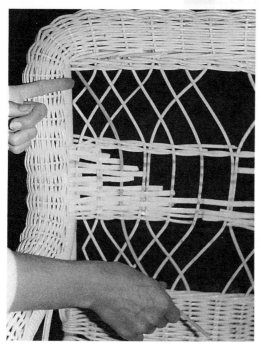

Soak the correct size of round reed until it is pliable. Insert the new spoke up through the weave (middle section). Remember to follow the pattern of the original spokes (leaning to the left or right), and insert the tips of the spokes about one inch into the rolled, hollow serpentine back.

After the spokes are glued into place, restore the horizontal under-and-over weave in the middle section. The flat reed for this is soaked to ensure flexibility and then woven onto the skeleton of spokes. The same method of locking is put to use here: the starting end of the new reed and the cut-off end of the old reed lie close together and form a fastening.

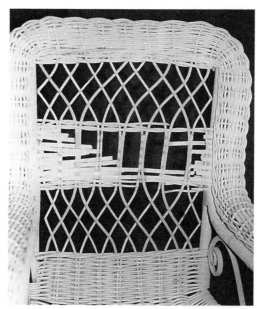

Glue all spokes into place and let the glue set for one hour. The spokes are the skeleton of any wicker piece, and should therefore be very secure before any weaving is attempted.

The finished job is now ready for painting.

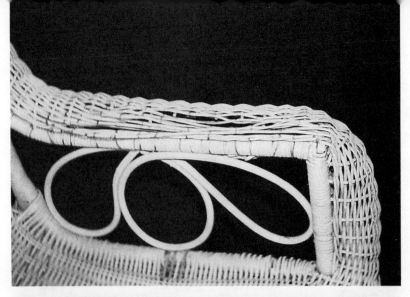

Hollow Serpentine Arms

A caved-in hollow serpentine arm is one of the most common flaws in old wicker furniture. Although these rounded arms were beautiful to look at, they were also usually the first part of the chair to be broken—simply because the arms are major stress points. All previous restoration techniques should be completely mastered before such a job is attempted.

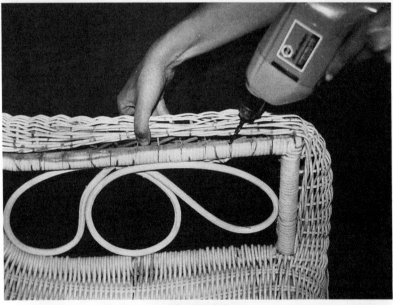

An electric drill should be used to make half-inch holes in the wooden framework. The original holes (some will still have the broken spokes inside) will show you where to drill. Be careful to use the right size bit, for the holes must be large enough for the new spokes to fit into snugly. Drill holes for all the spokes that need to be replaced.

After soaking the correct size of round reed until it is very pliable, insert the sharpened tip of a new spoke into the weave alongside the broken spoke. Carefully push it through the weave, using a screwdriver to guide it along from the top.

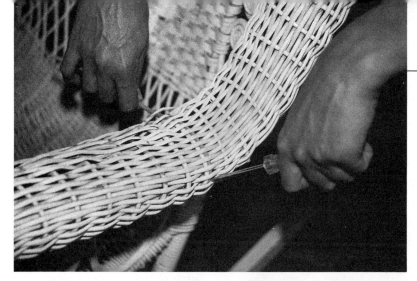

Continue the process until the new spoke is pushed completely around the arm.

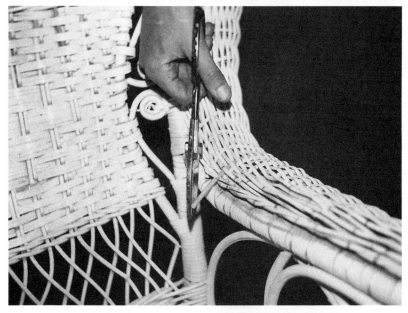

Now clip the other end of the new spoke at a slight angle to ensure easy insertion into the hole you have drilled for it.

In order to ensure a tight bond, fill the hole with white glue before inserting the spoke.

Carefully bend the spoke and fit it into the glue-filled hole. The spoke may have to be recut several times, to make it the proper length to match the height of the old spokes directly behind it. Also try to duplicate the curve of the arch of the original spokes.

When the new spoke has dried in place, clip off the old damaged spoke next to it and carefully pull it out.

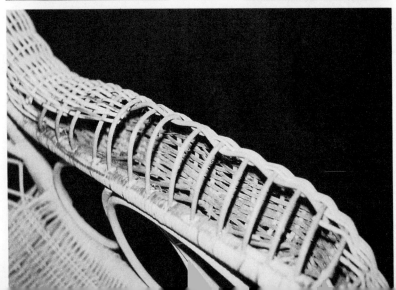

Repeat the steps until all the new spokes are in place and the glue has set. Now that the skeleton of spokes has been restored, weaving is the next step. First, clip the old woven horizontal reeds back so that they are all tucked in under one of the spokes.

Start weaving by locking the new reed under both the spoke and the end of the old reed.

When weaving, be careful not to put too much pressure on any of the spokes or they may be pulled out of the framework. It is helpful to brace the reed next to the spoke with one hand while guiding the end of the reed through the spokes with the other hand.

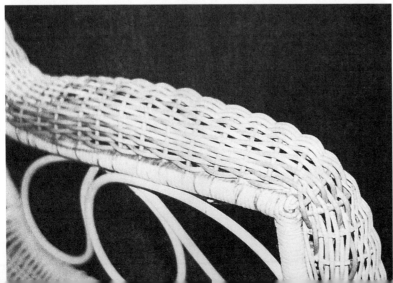

The finished arm should be covered with a thin coat of white glue to ensure durability as well as seal the porous reeds.

If you are interested in restoring your old wicker chair or settee completely, it is a good idea to learn how to install a prewoven, or set-in, cane seat. Over 90 percent of all wicker furniture made with cane seats had this type of set-in seat (developed by Watkins of Heywood Brothers and Company), to save on the high labor costs of hand caning. It is easy to determine whether or not any chair once had a set-in cane seat: if a series of small holes circles the seat opening, the chair was originally caned by hand, but if a groove runs around the perimeter of the seat, you can be sure the chair originally had a set-in cane seat.

INSTALLING A SET-IN CANE SEAT

REMOVING OLD CANE AND SPLINE

The first step in replacing set-in cane seats is to be sure that the surrounding groove is clean. More often than not, you will have to remove old cane and some leftover spline (a triangular-shaped reed that fits into the groove) with a wide chisel and a hammer. Place the chisel on the inner edge of the spline and tap carefully around the entire seat with a hammer, to loosen the spline from the frame. Repeat around the outside of the spline. After the spline is loosened, slowly lift it out with a screwdriver. Be very careful not to chip the wood around the groove.

Be sure that all the old cane, spline, and hardened glue are removed from the groove.

After the cane webbing has been soaked, place it over the seat with the glossy side up. Then, with the sharp-pointed wooden wedge, lightly tap a few inches of the cane into the groove at the back of the chair. Next, cut a temporary wedge of spline (about one inch in length) and drive it over the depressed cane and into the groove with the blunt-end wooden wedge. This piece of spline will serve as a temporary holding device. Repeat the same procedure at the front of the chair, so that the cane is pulled tight from the front to the back of the seat.

PREPARATION AND MATERIALS

Select spline that fits into the groove easily and can be removed with your fingers. If the spline does not fit into the groove smoothly, it will be too large when it dries. The seat used here has rounded corners, but some seats have square or mitered corners, and for these seats the spline should be installed in cut lengths.

Soak the prewoven cane in warm water for one hour to make it pliable, and then hang it on a hook for five minutes to drip dry. The spline should also be soaked, but for only fifteen minutes (just before you start work).

You will also need two wooden wedges—one with a sharp point to drive the cane into the groove, the other with a blunt end to hammer the spline into the groove without damaging the spline. Softwood is best to use if you are making these wedges yourself; hardwood can break the cane. (Wooden wedges, as well as the prewoven cane and the spline, can be ordered from the supply houses listed in Appendix 1.)

The following tools and related items are also necessary: a hammer, a mat knife, clippers, and white glue.

If you follow the illustrated step-by-step instructions, you should be able to install your own set-in cane seat.

After the two spline wedges are in place, take the sharp wooden wedge and—with a hammer—carefully tap down the cane webbing into the groove all around the seat until the outline of the groove can be seen clearly.

After the spline has been lightly hammered into the groove all around the seat, cut the end of it very carefully so that it will butt up against the other end of the spline at the back of the seat.

Remove the two small spline wedges from the front and back of the seat, and pour a small amount of white glue along the path of the groove. Using the blunt-end wooden wedge and the presoaked spline, begin to tap the spline into the groove.

When the entire length of spline has been inserted into the groove, use the mat knife to cut off the excess strands of cane around the outside. Take great care not to slice into the spline with the mat knife.

After the excess cane has been completely removed, go around the seat again with the blunt-end wedge and a hammer, pounding the spline into the groove until it is level with the wooden seat frame. Finally, pour glue along the length of the spline and work it in on both sides to ensure a tight bond. (Excess glue can be removed with a wet cloth.) Let the chair dry at normal room temperature for two days before you use it. Do not set it outdoors in the sun to dry.

CARE OF WICKER

CLEANING WICKER FURNITURE

Wicker is a low-maintenance antique. The best method of cleaning wicker furniture is to go over it thoroughly with a soft brush and warm soapy water. A toothbrush is recommended for hard-to-get-at places. Wicker pieces made of reed and willow (both natural and painted) should be periodically wiped off with a wet soft cloth. If this type of wicker becomes brittle, it should be taken outside and hosed off—the water will feed the reeds and ensure greater flexibility. On the other hand, a piece of wicker made of either fiber (twisted paper) or sea grass should never be hosed off, because water will weaken the weave as well as the individual fibers. To clean this type of wicker furniture use a damp cloth only.

Very diluted domestic bleach will whiten soiled reed and willow pieces that have been left in their natural state, but it should be used with great caution and only if scrubbing with warm soapy water does not do the job.

PRESERVING NATURAL WICKER

In referring to wicker furniture, the term "natural" designates any piece left unpainted. Originally, all so-called natural wicker was actually either stained or coated with a protective coat of clear varnish or lacquer. Natural wicker should be left unpainted whenever possible, because it is far more valuable than painted wicker; it will also withstand the weather better if used outdoors.

After cleaning natural wicker, you can maintain its natural color and give it a healthy sheen by applying linseed oil with a soft cloth. Periodic applications of this oil will also allow natural reeds to "breathe" and obtain the necessary moisture to keep the piece flexible.

STRIPPING PAINTED WICKER

Many people wonder if painted wicker can be stripped back to its natural state. The answer is yes—but with some reservations. Most wicker furniture made of reed, rattan, and willow can be successfully stripped of paint by a reliable professional furniture stripper. One key to success, however, is making sure that the material is not man-made fiber, for the chemicals in the stripper's hot tank will eat through that material in no time at all. By contrast, most other types of wicker furniture can be stripped of a dozen or more layers of paint without suffering permanent damage. The chemicals in the hot tank will sometimes raise small, whiskerlike fibers from the individual reeds, but these are easy to deal with. The most efficient way of removing them is to singe them off with a propane torch set at a low flame. Remember, always, that after wicker furniture has been stripped and allowed to dry out, to ensure flexibility it should be thoroughly hosed off with water. After drying completely, the piece should then be oiled, stained, or varnished according to taste.

REFINISHING NATURAL WICKER

Whether staining an entire wicker chair or a small repair job to match the existing finish, it is a wise first step to secure from your local hardware or paint dealer a booklet illustrating the use of stains and dyes on various materials. Because it is important to stain a piece with a substance that is compatible with the original finish, it is always a good idea to try a little of any new stain on a hidden area, then wait for results before going ahead with the entire job. Sometimes different stains react against each other and cracks or blisters develop. Even if this happens, the piece will not be ruined if the test was made in a hidden area. Should the first stain prove incompatible, test another one that has a different chemical base. When you have found a stain that is compatible with the original, apply several thin coats, slowly darkening the stain with each application until the desired depth of color is obtained.

Because of its porosity, wicker furniture soils very easily unless some type of clear finish is used as a sealer. The best way to finish it is to apply one or two light coats of a good grade of varnish. Spray finishing, using either a commercial aerosol can or a compressor, is the best method of evenly distributing a varnish, shellac, or clear lacquer finish on wicker furniture.

PAINTING WICKER

The worst thing you can do to a piece of natural wicker is paint it. Quality antique natural wicker is increasingly rare and should be looked upon as a true art form. Painting should be avoided at all costs. There is an abundance of painted wicker available on today's market to choose from without destroying a natural piece.

Victorian oblong table with birdcage design and stick-and-ball work.

The sad fact is that most antique wicker furniture has been painted one color or another. White and some shade of green or brown were among the favorite colors of years past. Today many people choose to repaint wicker furniture because of personal preference or to match the color of a specific room. If you decide to repaint your wicker, do so with care.

Cleaning and preparation are the key elements in doing a successful paint job on wicker furniture. All dirt and dust should be removed from the piece before painting begins (see "Cleaning Wicker Furniture, above). Some of the older pieces, especially those that were used outdoors, were painted every year. Since this annual summer ritual of painting was fairly common in the past, some old wicker can bear dozens of coats of globbed-on paint. When the existing paint is chipped or flaking, try to remove any loose flakes with a stiff brush. Some careful spot sanding with extra-fine sandpaper can be an effective finishing touch before you start repainting.

Combination ottoman/hamper with diamond design on the top and sides from the turn of the century.

It is extremely difficult—sometimes impossible—to paint wicker successfully with a brush, and so I strongly recommend spray painting. If you are doing only one or two small pieces, use a high-grade commercial spray paint in an aerosol can (gloss lacquer or enamel) in order to cut costs. It is especially important, when using canned spray paint, to get a strong, steady spray. The best way to ensure this is to shake the can vigorously for three or four minutes before using and keep the spray nozzle clean of any paint buildup (use a pin to unclog the hole).

When painting more than just a couple of pieces of wicker, use a compressor for a professional-quality job. Although it takes more time to use a compressor, and the cost is significantly higher than for using a spray can, the results are truly worth the extra effort and expense if you want a long-lasting, high-quality job. For the compressor paint job, get a high-grade acrylic enamel paint (Sherwin-Williams is recommended) and an enamel reducing compound to thin it out (three parts enamel to one part reducer).

The actual painting should be done outdoors in dry, warm weather. It is best to spray the underside of a piece first, then turn it right side up to complete the job. The most important rules in spray painting wicker furniture are: Use several thin coats rather than a single heavy one. Allow each coat to dry completely before applying the next one. There is far less chance for unsightly drips to accumulate if you follow these simple rules.

Fancy reception chair from the late Victorian era.

APPENDIX 1
CRAFT SUPPLY HOUSES

Because most general craft shops carry a limited selection of wicker repair materials, I would advise sending a small sample of the material you wish to duplicate to one of the following mail-order craft supply houses. The owners of these companies are very helpful, and most will tell you what the material is, how much it will cost, and how to order it through their illustrated catalogs.

CANE & BASKET SUPPLY
  COMPANY
1283 South Cochran Avenue
Los Angeles, California 90019

CONNECTICUT CANE & REED
  COMPANY
P.O. Box 1276
Manchester, Connecticut 06040

CHARLES SCHOBER COMPANY
2024 North 2d Street
Philadelphia, Pennsylvania 19122

ABLE TO CANE
67 Main Street

P.O. Box 429 (AD)
Warren, Maine 04864

CANE SHOP
15635 Madison Avenue
Cleveland, Ohio 44107

FRANK'S CANE & RUSH SUPPLY
7244 Heil Avenue
Huntington Beach, California 92647

PEERLESS RATTAN & REED
  MFG. CO.
222 Lake Avenue
P.O. Box 636
Yonkers, New York 10702

THE H. H. PERKINS COMPANY
10 South Bradley Road
Woodbridge, Connecticut 06525

BERSTED'S
521 West 10th Avenue
Box 40
Monmouth, Illinois 61462

THE WICKER SHOP
2190 Marshall Avenue
St. Paul, Minnesota 55104

< 223 >

Half-round sewing basket with open figure-eight loop design from the turn of the century.

APPENDIX 2
WICKER RESTORATION SPECIALISTS

ALABAMA

D & H CRAFTED FURNISHINGS
Route 6, Box 39
Decatur, Alabama 35603

ALLEN'S ANTIQUES
121 Telegraph Road
Chickasaw, Alabama 36611

ARIZONA

THE SEAT WEAVING SHOP
2238 North 24th Street
Phoenix, Arizona 85008

ARKANSAS

CHARLOTTE THOMPSON
1544 Crestwood
North Little Rock, Arkansas 72116

CALIFORNIA

WINDSOR'S CANE & WICKER
  REPAIR
130 East 17th Street, Suite G
Costa Mesa, California 92627

THE HAYS HOUSE OF WICKER
8565 Melrose Avenue
Los Angeles, California 90069
(213) 652-1999

LEW TUT
2615 South El Camino Real
San Mateo, California 94401

COLORADO

GLEE & GINNY MOORE
11250 Highway 50
P.O. Box 112
Manzanola, Colorado 81058

CONNECTICUT

THE WICKER FIXER
Connecticut Antique Wicker
1052 Main Street, Rear
Newington, Connecticut 06111

ABLE TO CANE
New Haven, Connecticut
(203) 624-1141

GEORGIA

HEIRLOOM WICKER
709 Miami Circle
Atlanta, Georgia 30324
(404) 233-6333

ILLINOIS

THE COLLECTED WORKS
905 Ridge Road

Wilmette, Illinois 60091
(312) 251-1120

INDIANA

THOMAS DUNCAN
P.O. Box 481
Syracuse, Indiana 46567
(219) 457-5647

ANTIQUE REPAIR SHOPPE
7222 Magoun Avenue
Hammond, Indiana 46324

IOWA

BELDINGS FURNITURE
    RESTORATION
2734 Mt. Vernon Road S.E.
Cedar Rapids, Iowa 52403

LOUISIANA

THE WICKER GAZEBO
3137 Magazine Street
New Orleans, Louisiana 70115

MAINE

CALENDAR COURT ANTIQUES
Route 35
Kennebunkport, Maine 04043

ABLE TO CANE
67 Main Street
P.O. Box 429 (AD)
Warren, Maine 04864

MARYLAND

THE WICKER LADY OF
    MARYLAND
505 Jumpers Hole Road
Severna Park, Maryland 21146

WHIPPEE'S WICKER
523 Herring Avenue
Fairhaven, Maryland 20754

MEADOWS ANTIQUES
Baltimore, Maryland 21202
(301) 837-5427

MASSACHUSETTS

THE WICKER PORCH
335 Wareham Road
Route 6
Marion, Massachusetts 02738
(508) 748-3606
    Mailing address:
    P.O. Box 47
    East Wareham, Massachusetts
    02538
    Residence phone: (508) 748-0962

THE WICKER PORCH II
13 North Water Street
Nantucket Island, Massachusetts 02554
(508) 228-1052

THE WICKER LADY
1197 Walnut Street
Newton Highlands, Massachusetts
    02161
(617) 964-7490

MINNESOTA

AN ELEGANT PLACE
421 Third Street
Excelsior, Minnesota 55331

THE WICKER SHOP
2190 Marshall Avenue
St. Paul, Minnesota 55104

MISSOURI

THE WICKER FIXER
Route 1, Box 283-B
Ozark, Missouri 65721

NEW JERSEY

DOVETAIL ANTIQUES
White Pine Road
R.R. 2, Box 194
Columbus, New Jersey 08022
(609) 298-5245

NEW YORK

ROUND LAKE ANTIQUES
Route 9, Box 358
Round Lake, New York 12151

LET BYGONES BE!
59 Sea Cliff Avenue
Glen Cove, New York 11542

BUCKBOARD ANTIQUES
Box 129-08
Wallkill, New York 12589

T & T WICKER
Rt. 12B, P.O. Box 894
Deansboro, New York 13328

NORTH CAROLINA

CLARA'S ANTIQUES
1525 East Independence Boulevard
Charlotte, North Carolina 28205

OHIO

THE WICKER WIZARD
415 Superior Street
Rossford, Ohio 43460
(419) 666-9461

WACKY WICKER WORKERS
Antiques of Chester
7976 Mayfield Road
Chesterland, Ohio 44026
(216) 255-1172

THE WICKER PICKER
530 East Philadelphia Avenue
Youngstown, Ohio 44502

OREGON

SUE KAADY
Riverside Villa
18758 S.E. River Road, #58
Milwaukie, Oregon 97267

PENNSYLVANIA

CAROLYN VOLK
240 Neely School Road
Wexford, Pennsylvania 15090

RHODE ISLAND

BENTON'S WICKER
At Blackstone Place
727 East Avenue
Pawtucket, Rhode Island 02860

TEXAS

THE OLD WICKER GARDEN
4617 Cole Avenue
Dallas, Texas 75205

WHIPPOORWILL WICKER WORKS
811 West Avenue
San Antonio, Texas 78201

CAROLINE'S CANING AND
    WICKER REPAIR
3806 Alisa Ann
Corpus Christi, Texas 78418

VIRGINIA

THE VICTORIAN REVIVAL
7500 Idylwood Road
Falls Church, Virginia 22043

MR. WHISKER'S ATTIC
6315 Fairview Drive
Mechanicsville, Virginia 23111

MR. AND MRS. WILLIAM D.
    CRITZER
773 Oyster Point Road
Newport News, Virginia 23602

WASHINGTON

WICKER DESIGN ANTIQUES
515 15th E.
Seattle, Washington 98112

WISCONSIN

COUNTRY WEAVERS
1014 Harrison Street
Black River Falls, Wisconsin 54615

Turn of the century rocker with rolled arms in cornucopia design with inset curlicues and spools set into back and skirting wrapped with fine round reed.

APPENDIX 3
ANTIQUE WICKER SPECIALTY SHOPS

ALABAMA

ALLEN'S ANTIQUES
121 Telegraph Road
Chickasaw, Alabama 36611

ARIZONA

THE SEAT WEAVING SHOP
2238 North 24th Street
Phoenix, Arizona 85008

CALIFORNIA

ARABESQUE ANTIQUES
417 Trout Gulch Road
Aptos, California 95003
(408) 688-9883

THE HAYS HOUSE OF WICKER
8565 Melrose Avenue
Los Angeles, California 90069
(213) 652-1999

SERENDIPITY
108 F Street
Eureka, California 95501

CONNECTICUT

A SUMMER PLACE
On the Green
Guilford, Connecticut 06437
(203) 453-5153

CONNECTICUT ANTIQUE WICKER
1052 Main Street, Rear
Newington, Connecticut 06111

GEORGIA

HEIRLOOM WICKER
709 Miami Circle
Atlanta, Georgia 30324
(404) 233-6333

WICKERWILL ANTIQUES
3519 Broad Street
Chamblee, Georgia 30341

ILLINOIS

THE COLLECTED WORKS
905 Ridge Road
Wilmette, Illinois 60091
(312) 251-1120

THE WICKER WITCH OF
   CHICAGO
2146 West Belmont
Chicago, Illinois 60618

INDIANA

WICKER & THINGS
2032 Broadway
Fort Wayne, Indiana 46804

LOUISIANA

THE WICKER GAZEBO
3137 Magazine Street
New Orleans, Louisiana 70115

MAINE

CALENDAR COURT ANTIQUES
Route 35
Kennebunkport, Maine 04043

OXBOW FARM ANTIQUES
Route 1
Lincolnville Beach, Maine 04849

MARYLAND

JOAN M. COLE WICKER
Potomac, Maryland 20851
(301) 983-1805

WHIPPEE'S WICKER
523 Herring Avenue
Fairhaven, Maryland 20754

MEADOWS ANTIQUES
Baltimore, Maryland 21202
(301) 837-5427

MASSACHUSETTS

THE WICKER PORCH
335 Wareham Road
Route 6
Marion, Massachusetts 02738
(508) 748-3606
    Mailing address:
    P.O. Box 47
    East Wareham, Massachusetts
        02538
    (508) 748-0962

THE WICKER PORCH II
13 North Water Street
Nantucket Island, Massachusetts 02554
(508) 228-1052

THE WICKER LADY
1197 Walnut Street
Newton Highlands, Massachusetts
    02161
(617) 964-7490

WICKER UNLIMITED
108 Washington Street
Marblehead, Massachusetts 01945

CORNER HOUSE ANTIQUES
Corner of Main and Old Mill Pond
    (Route 7)
Sheffield, Massachusetts 01257

VANWORTH ANTIQUES
At the Common (Routes 2A & 110)
Littleton Common, Massachusetts
    01460

MINNESOTA

AN ELEGANT PLACE
421 Third Street
Excelsior, Minnesota 55331

THE WICKER SHOP
2190 Marshall Avenue
St. Paul, Minnesota 55104

AMERICAN CLASSICS
4944 Xerxes S.
Minneapolis, Minnesota 55410

NEW JERSEY

DOVETAIL ANTIQUES
White Pine Road
R.R. 2, Box 194
Columbus, New Jersey 08022
(609) 298-5245

NEW YORK

ROUND LAKE ANTIQUES
Route 9, Box 358
Round Lake, New York 12151

LET BYGONES BE!
59 Sea Cliff Avenue
Glen Cove, New York 11542

THE GAZEBO
660 Madison Avenue
New York, New York 10021

BUCKBOARD ANTIQUES
Box 129-08
Wallkill, New York 12589

TED MEYER'S HARBOR ANTIQUES
Montauk Highway
Wainscott, New York 11975

CIRCA 1890
265 East 78th Street
New York, New York 10021

OHIO

THE WACKY WICKER WORKERS
Antiques of Chester
7976 Mayfield Road
Chesterland, Ohio 44026
(216) 255-1172

WICKERING HEIGHTS
415 Superior Street
Rossford, Ohio 43460
(419) 666-9461

GIBSON-GIRL MEMORIES
625 Main Street E.
Toledo, Ohio 43605

OREGON

POSSIBILITIES ANTIQUES
1249 Commercial S.E.
Salem, Oregon 97302

PENNSYLVANIA

APPLEGATE ANTIQUES
100 Lincoln Way East
New Oxford, Pennsylvania 17350
(717) 624-2137

RHODE ISLAND

BENTON'S WICKER
At Blackstone Place
727 East Avenue
Pawtucket, Rhode Island 02860

TEXAS

THE OLD WICKER GARDEN
4617 Cole Avenue
Dallas, Texas 75205

WHIPPOORWILL WICKER WORKS
811 West Avenue
San Antonio, Texas 78201

VIRGINIA

MR. AND MRS. WILLIAM D.
  CRITZER
773 Oyster Point Road
Newport News, Virginia 23602

MR. WHISKER'S ATTIC
6315 Fairview Drive
Mechanicsville, Virginia 23111

THE VICTORIAN REVIVAL
7500 Idylwood Road
Falls Church, Virginia 22043

WASHINGTON

WICKER DESIGN ANTIQUES
515 15th E.
Seattle, Washington 98112

CANADA

SUSAN'S ANTIQUES
585 Mt. Pleasant Road
Toronto, Ontario M4S 2M5
Canada

Magazine table from the late 1920s.

APPENDIX 4

MANUFACTURERS AND NOTABLE RETAILERS OF COLLECTIBLE WICKER FURNITURE

< 233 >

CHICAGO REEDWARE
MANUFACTURING COMPANY
(Chicago, Illinois)

CHINA SEA GRASS FURNITURE &
RUGS

CHITTENDEN-EASTMAN
COMPANY
(Burlington, Iowa)

JOHN A. COLBY & SON
(Chicago, Illinois)

THE COLSON CHAIR COMPANY
(Elyria, Ohio)

COLT WILLOW WARE WORKS
(Hartford, Connecticut)

CRAFTSMAN FURNITURE
(Eastwood, New York)

A. CUMMINGS
(New York City)

CUNNINGHAM REED AND
RATTAN COMPANY
(New York City)

D

F. DEBSKI
(New York City)

P. DERBY & COMPANY
(Gardner, Massachusetts)

DERICHS + SAVERTEIG
(Coburg, Germany)

J. A. DICKERMAN AND COMPANY

DOWNING CARRIAGE COMPANY
(Erie, Pennsylvania)

DRYAD WORKS
(Leicestershire, England)

E

ELLMORE
(Thurmaston, Leicestershire, England)

F

FICKS REED COMPANY
(New York City)

FORD & JOHNSON COMPANY
(Chicago, Illinois)

FORD-JOHNSON FIBRE RUSH
FURNITURE
(Michigan City, Indiana)

G

GENDRON IRON WHEEL
COMPANY
(Toledo, Ohio)

GIBBS CHAIR COMPANY
(Kankakee, Illinois)

THE GRAND CENTRAL WICKER
SHOP
(New York City)

GRAND RAPIDS FIBER CORD
COMPANY
(Grand Rapids, Michigan)

H

HANDCRAFT FURNITURE
COMPANY
(Lincoln, Nebraska)

HARRISON AND SONS
(Grantham, England)

HARTFORD CHAIR COMPANY
(Hartford, Connecticut)

HEDSTROM UNION COMPANY
(Gardner, Massachusetts)

WALTER HEYWOOD CHAIR
COMPANY
(New York City)

HEYWOOD BROTHERS AND
COMPANY
(Gardner, Massachusetts)

HEYWOOD BROTHERS AND
WAKEFIELD COMPANY
(Gardner, Massachsuetts)

HEYWOOD-MORRILL RATTAN
COMPANY
(Gardner, Massachusetts)

HEYWOOD-WAKEFIELD
COMPANY
(Gardner, Massachusetts)

DEAN HICKS

HIGH POINT BENDING AND
CHAIR COMPANY
(Silver City, North Carolina)

HUNTINGDON RATTAN & REED
COMPANY

J

JENKINS-PHIPPS
(Wakefield, Massachusetts)

JOHNSON-RANDALL COMPANY
(Traverse City, Michigan)

JONES-SMITH
(New York City)

K

KALTEX FURNITURE COMPANY
(Jackson, Michigan)

KARPEN BROTHERS
(Chicago)

KARPEN GUARANTEED
    CONSTRUCTION FURNITURE
(Chicago and New York City)

KELLY BROTHERS
(Gardner, Massachusetts)

THE KINLEY MANUFACTURING
    COMPANY
(Chicago, Illinois)

L

THE LARKIN COMPANY
(Buffalo, New York)

LARKINS & COMPANY
(San Francisco, California)

LEADER
(Gardner, Massachusetts)

LLOYD MANUFACTURING
    COMPANY
(Menominee, Michigan)

LONG BEACH REED & WILLOW
    FURNITURE COMPANY
(New York City)

THE LUBURG MANUFACTURING
    COMPANY
(Philadelphia, Pennsylvania)

W. LUSTY & SONS LTD.
(London, England)

M

MADEWELL CHAIR COMPANY
(Sheboygan, Wisconsin)

MADISON BASKETCRAFT
    COMPANY
(Burlington, Iowa)

MANHATTAN WICKER COMPANY
(New York City)

MASTERCRAFT REED COMPANY

MCGIBBON & COMPANY
(New York City)

JOSEPH P. McHIGH & COMPANY
(New York City)

A. MEINECKE & SON
(Milwaukee, Wisconsin)

MENTZER REED COMPANY
(Grand Rapids, Michigan)

MERIKORD—AMERICAN CHAIR
    COMPANY
(Sheboygan, Wisconsin)

METROPOLITAN CHAIR
    COMPANY
(Hartford, Connecticut)

MIDLAND CHAIR AND SEATING
    COMPANY
(Michigan City, Indiana)

MINNET & COMPANY

MONTGOMERY WARD COMPANY

MURPHY OF MICHIGAN
(Gardner, Massachusetts)

N

N.E.P. COMPANY
(Boston, Massachusetts)

NEWBURGH REED COMPANY
(Newburgh, New York)

NEW ENGLAND CHAIR COMPANY
(Hartford, Connecticut)

NEW ENGLAND REED COMPANY
(Boston, Massachusetts)

NEW HAVEN CHAIR COMPANY
(New Haven, Connecticut)

NEW YORK STATE HOUSE OF
    REFUGE
(New York City)

NIAGARA REED COMPANY
(Buffalo, New York)

M. A. NICOLAI
(Dresden, Germany)

NORTHFIELD FURNITURE
    COMPANY
(Sheboygan, Wisconsin)

NOVELTY RATTAN COMPANY
(Boston and Chicago)

O

A. H. ORDWAY AND COMPANY
(South Framingham, Massachusetts)

OREGON CHAIR COMPANY

P

PACIFIC COAST RATTAN
    COMPANY
(San Francisco and Oakland,
    California)

PAINE'S FURNITURE COMPANY
(Boston, Massachusetts)

PEABODY & WHITNEY
(Leominster, Massachusetts)

PECK & HILLS FURNITURE
    COMPANY
(New York City)

PIAGET-DONNELLY COMPANY
(Grand Rapids, Michigan)

PIONEER

PRAG-RUDNIKER
(Poland)

PRAIRIE GRASS FURNITURE
COMPANY, INC.
(Glendale, Long Island, New York)

THE PURITAN COMPANY
(Gardner, Massachusetts)

R

G. W. RANDALL & COMPANY
(Grand Rapids, Michigan)

THE REED SHOP

REEDCRAFT, INC.
(Baldwinville, Massachusetts)

REEDCRAFT FURNITURE
COMPANY
(Chicago and Los Angeles)

REEDFIBRE
(Iona, Michigan)

THEODOR REIMANN
(Dresden, Germany)

THE BEMIS RIDDELL FIBRE
COMPANY
(Sheboygan, Wisconsin)

ROCKRIDGE WICKER WORKS
(Oakland, California)

RUSTIC HICKORY COMPANY
(Indianapolis, Indiana)

S

SARGENT MANUFACTURING
COMPANY
(Chicago, Illinois)

CHARLES SCHOBER & COMPANY
(Philadelphia, Pennsylvania)

SEARS, ROEBUCK AND COMPANY
(Chicago, Illinois)

SHEBOYGAN REED AND FIBER
FURNITURE COMPANY
(Sheboygan, Wisconsin)

LUDWIG SILD
(Vienna, Austria)

W. & J. SLOANE
(New York City)

SPEAR & COMPANY
(Pittsburgh, Pennsylvania)

THE GUSTAV STICKLEY COMPANY
(Eastwood, New York)

STICKLEY-BRANDT FURNITURE
COMPANY
(Binghamton, New York)

SUNREED-HORACE MILLS LTD.
(Newark-on-Trent, England)

SUSSEX COMPANY
(New York City)

T

A. A. TISDALE & COMPANY
(Leominster, Massachusetts)

TOPF & COMPANY
(New York City)

TUNG MOW FURNITURE
COMPANY
(Hong Kong, China)

U

UHRAN CARRIAGE COMPANY
(Rochester, New York)

V

VALLEY CITY RATTAN COMPANY
(Grand Rapids, Michigan)

J. B. VAN SHRIVER COMPANY
(Camden, New Jersey)

A. A. VANTINE & COMPANY, INC.
(New York City)

W

WAKEFIELD RATTAN COMPANY
(Wakefield, Massachusetts)

WAKEFIELD REED CHAIRS &
CARRIAGE COMPANY
(Wakefield, Massachusetts)

JOHN WANAMAKER
(Philadelphia, Pennsylvania)

W. B. WASHBURN COMPANY
(Erving, Massachusetts)

WASHBURN-HEYWOOD CHAIR
COMPANY
(Boston, Massachusetts)

F. A. WHITNEY CARRIAGE
COMPANY
(Leominster, Massachusetts)

W. F. WHITNEY & COMPANY
(South Ashburnam, Massachusetts)

WHITNEY REED CHAIR COMPANY
(Leominster, Massachusetts)

WICKER-KRAFT COMPANY
(Newburgh, New York)

WILLOWCRAFT
(Cambridge, Massachusetts)

WILLOW & REED
(Brooklyn, New York)

Y

YPSILANTI REED FURNITURE
COMPANY
(Ionia, Michigan)

Glossary

Arabesques.   An intricate wickerwork pattern that interlaces flowers and other flowing designs. Strictly for ornamentation and most often found in Victorian wicker.

Bar Harbor style.   Open-weave reed and willow pieces that became popular in the early 1900s through the twenties. This style made use of round reed latticework to lessen the cost of hand labor.

Binder cane.   Cane that is slightly wider and thicker than the normal chair-seating variety. Most often used as a structural wrap on wicker furniture.

Birdcage design.   A typically Victorian wicker design, which, due to its unique arrangement of bowed vertical reeds, seemed to "cage" a cane-wrapped leg or back brace.

Braiding.   Long section of reeds or fiber that have been braided together in the traditional three-way style.

Cane.   The outer bark of the rattan palm, which is sliced off in long thin strips. The resilient, glossy material became popular in Europe during the seventeenth century, when it was woven into the seats and backs of chairs.

Cane webbing.   This machine-made webbing (sometimes called sheet cane) is woven from natural cane and used for set-in cane seating.

Curlicue.   A circular, coil-like design employed in many Victorian and early 1900s wicker pieces for ornamentation.

Elliptic springs.   Heavy-duty ellipse-shaped metal springs, often used on Victorian platform rockers and baby carriages.

Fiber.   Sometimes spelled "fibre," in the past this man-made (and chemically treated) twisted paper was made to resemble real twisted bulrushes.

Gesso.   Plaster of Paris prepared with glue for use in making bas-reliefs. On wicker furniture this molded fancywork often utilized rose and wreath designs.

Hand-caned seat.   Any caned seat woven by hand rather than machine. On hand-caned seating the holes in the bottom of the seat should be clearly visible.

Mission style.   A style of wicker furniture design that appeared on the scene around 1900 and made use of straight-lined, practical designs.

Natural wicker.   Any wicker left unpainted.

Oriental sea grass.   A natural twine material twisted to resemble rope. It is variegated green and tan in color and turns light brown with age.

Osiers.   Supple twigs from willow trees, which are peeled and soaked before being used in the making of willow furniture.

Photographer's chair.   Sometimes called posing chairs or fancy reception chairs, these extremely ornate pieces were used in Victorian portrait photography studios.

Platform rocker.   Wicker platform rockers were designed to prevent rug wear and were attached by powerful metal springs (usually coil or elliptic) to a stationary base.

Rattan.   A climbing palm native to the East Indies. It is from the rattan palm that we obtain cane (its outer coating) and reed (its inner pith).

Reed.   The pliable inner pith of the rattan palm. First used in the 1850s, reed is the most common of the materials used in the construction of wicker furniture.

Rosette.   A circular roselike design most often decorating the arm tips of Victorian chairs, rockers, and settees.

Rush.   A natural grasslike, leafless stem derived from the sedge family. Rush was sometimes used in combination with other materials in wicker furniture. Most often it was used for seats in nonwicker chairs.

Scrollwork.   A flowing series of curlicues or other fancywork that resembles breaking waves.

Serpentine design.   A curved, hollow, rolled-edge technique employed in many Victorian and early 1900s wicker pieces to finish off edges and soften harsh angles.

Set-in cane seat.   Sometimes called prewoven cane, the sheet cane webbing was made on a loom. An automatic channeling machine cut out a small groove around the wooden seat frame to allow the webbing to be attached to the shallow channel by means of a triangular-shaped reed called spline.

Spokes.   The vertical reeds over which wickerwork is woven.

Wicker.   An umbrella term that describes all woven furniture made with such materials as rattan, reed, cane, willow, fiber, sea grass, rush, raffia, and numerous dried grasses.

Willow.   These highly flexible twigs are blond-colored in their natural state and often exhibit small knots where tiny offshoots were removed. Willow resembles reed, especially when painted.

Fancy reception chair made by Heywood Brothers and Wakefield Company.

ACKNOWLEDGMENTS

It is a pleasure to be able to express my special appreciation to Frank Stagg, a true pioneer in the wicker revival. Sincere thanks also go to Mary Jean McLaughlin, Frank McNamee, Harry and Louise Olsson, Gert Patterson, Mike Bradbury, Judy Stoycheff, Bill and Lee Stewart, Lynn Wesch, Jerry Carnes, Nancy Gibson, Steven and Tammy Mottet, Mike and Vickie Owen, Jim and Marian Redmond, and Pete and Susan Tanzini for allowing me to photograph their extensive collections of wicker furniture; and to William Frohmader, Gary Denys, and Melissa McLaughlin for their expert photographic contributions.

I am also grateful to the efficient and courteous staffs of the Wakefield Historical Society; the Heywood-Wakefield Company; the Ohio Historical Society; the Beinecke Rare Book and Manuscript Library at Yale University; the Sonoma County Library in Santa Rosa, California; and the Pacific Grove Public Library in Pacific Grove, California.

And I would especially like to thank my agent, Susan Urstadt, and my editor, Ann Cahn, and Deborah Kerner and Nancy Maynes at Crown.

BIBLIOGRAPHY

Baker, Hollis S. *Furniture in the Ancient World: Origins and Evolution, 3100–475 B.C.* New York: Macmillan, 1966.

Lady Barker. *The Bedroom and Boudoir.* London: Macmillan, 1878.

Eaton, Lilley. *Genealogical History of the Town of Reading.* Boston: Mudge, 1874.

Greenwood, Richard N. *The Five Heywood Brothers (1826–1951): A Brief History of the Heywood-Wakefield Company During 125 Years.* New York: Newcomen Publications, 1951.

Walker, Francis A., ed. *International Exhibition: Reports and Awards,* vol. 4. Washington: Government Printing Office, 1880.

PHOTOGRAPH CREDITS

Arabesque Antiques: p. 33 bottom right, 81 top right, 99 top left, bottom left, 134 bottom, 176 bottom, 185 top, 187.

Dovetail Antiques: p. 77 left, 80 top right, 86 left, 89 top right, 90 bottom right, 96 bottom right, 97 right, 104 bottom right, 106 right, 111 right, 129 right, 133 top right, 139, 146, 183 right, 194, 198 top left, 224, 228.

An Elegant Place: p. 44, 101 top left, 109 top right, 136 bottom left, 137 top left, top right, 138, 141 top left, 142 top, 158 top, 164 bottom left, 177 left, 178 top, bottom, 179 top right, 182 bottom left, 193 bottom right.

Gibson-Girl Memories: p. 104 top left, 132 bottom, far left, left, 143 bottom right, 181 top right, 191 top left.

Hays House of Wicker: p. 177 top right.

Frank Stagg: p. ii, iv, 52 top, 54 top right, 56 top, bottom, 58 right, 60 bottom left, 61, 62 bottom, 63 top left, top right, bottom center, bottom right, 64 bottom right, left, 65 top right, bottom right, 66 top right, 67 bottom, 68 bottom, 69 top right, 88 bottom left, 103 bottom, 117 bottom right, 133 bottom far left, 138 top right, 145 bottom, 147 top left, 171 top left, top far right, bottom left, right, 173 top far left, top left, 180 top left, 196 top left.

Beverly Stephenson: p. 54 left, 59 top right, 65 bottom left, 169 top left, 199 right.

A Summer Place: p. 5, 42, 52 bottom, 67, 68 top, center left, center right, 69 top left, bottom left, bottom right, 71 bottom right, top right, 72 top left, bottom left, right, 73 top right, bottom right, 75, 76 top left, right, bottom left, 78 top right, top left, bottom right, bottom left, 79 bottom left, 82–83 top, bottom, 83 top, bottom, 84 top left, bottom left, 85 top, center, 87 top left, 88 top, bottom right, 89 top right, bottom right, 90 top left,

top right, bottom left, 91 right, top, 92 top right, bottom right, top left, bottom left, 93 top left, bottom left, top right, bottom right, 96 bottom left, 98, 100 top left, bottom, top right, 101 right, top center, bottom left, 102 top right, bottom right, bottom left, bottom center, top left, 103 right, 105 bottom, 106 top left, bottom left, 107 top left, bottom left, right, 108 top left, bottom left, top right, bottom right, 118 left, 126 right, top left, 127 bottom, 128 top, 133 bottom left, 134 top, 136 top left, 140 left, top right, bottom right, 143 top, bottom left, 144 top left, top right, bottom left, bottom right, 145 top, 147 right, 172 top left, 179 top left, bottom, 180 top right, 181 top left, 182 top left, right, 183 bottom right, top left, 184, 185 bottom, 188 bottom left, 189 top right, bottom right, 190, 191 bottom left, 192 bottom right, 193 left, top right, 197 bottom left, top right, 202 top left, 221 top right, 239, 242.

Wacky Wicker Workers: p. 9, 96 center, 112 left, 129 left, 135 top, bottom, 136 top right, 137 bottom left, 141 bottom, 176 top, 181 bottom, 184 bottom left, bottom right, 186 top far left, 188 top, 192 top right, 200, 201 right.

Wakefield Historical Society: p. 21, 22, 43, 45, 46, 47, 48, 49, 50 top, bottom, 51, 124 left, right, 125 left, right, 160, 161, 162 top, bottom right, 163.

Lynn Wesch: p. 70, 74 top right, bottom left, 80 left, 81 left, bottom right, 82 top, bottom, 84 right, 87 bottom left, 94 left, right, 95, 99 right, 109 left, 119, 130, 138 bottom right, 147 bottom left, 203 bottom right, 222, 232.

Whippoorwill Wicker Shoppe: p. 41, 79 top left, 96 top left, top right, 131 top, 164–165 (lamp), 175, 177 bottom right, 180 bottom, 186 bottom.

The Wicker Porch: p. 66 bottom right, 89 bottom left, 131 center, 136 bottom right, 165 top right.

The Metropolitan Museum of Art: p. 3.

Fairchild Tropical Garden: p. 7.

Century House: p. 4.

Staatliche Museum, Berlin: p. 10.

Cliches des Musees Nationaux, Paris: p. 8.

Rheinisches Landesmuseum Trier: p. 13.

The Royal Commission on Historical Monuments, England: p. 14.

North Carolina Museum of Art: p. 17.

Richard N. Greenwood: p. 20, 153.

Mike York: p. 53 bottom left.

Alice M. Saare: p. 64 top right.

Carol Wrathall: p. 66 bottom left.

The Collected Works: p. 103 top left.

Union Pacific Railroad Museum Collection: p. 122.

Carnes/Gibson, Private: p. 142 bottom.

Windsor's Cane & Wicker Repair: p. 77 top right, 128 bottom.

Jean Newhart's Antiques: p. 220 bottom left.

Serendipity Antiques: p. 97 left.

The Beinecke Rare Book and Manuscript Library, Yale University: p. 36.

Ohio Historical Society: p. 39 bottom left, bottom right, top left, top right, 40.

John Hathaway: p. 54 bottom right, 55, 58 top left, 167 top left.

Atlanta Historical Society: p. 30.

A Completed Century: p. 32, 150–151 bottom, 156–157 bottom.

Sears, Roebuck and Company: p. 120, 121, 148.

COLOR INSERT

A Summer Place: p. 1, 2, 3, 4 top right, 5 top left, top right, bottom left, bottom right, 6, 7, 8.

Wacky Wicker Workers: p. 4 left, right center, right bottom, 5 right center.

Sewing basket from the Heywood Brothers and Wakefield Company.

Index